■SCHOLASTIC

The Primary Teacher's Guide to

Financial Education

• Key subject knowledge • Background information • Teaching tips •

Anthony David

◩ SCHOLASTIC

Book End, Range Road, Witney, Oxfordshire, OX29 0YD
www.scholastic.co.uk
© 2013 Scholastic Ltd

1 2 3 4 5 6 7 8 9   3 4 5 6 7 8 9 0 1 2

British Library Cataloguing-in-Publication Data
A catalogue record for this book is available from the
British Library.

ISBN 978-1407-12799-6
Printed and bound by CPI Group (UK) Ltd, Croydon,
CR0 4YY

Author
Anthony David

Commissioning Editor
Paul Naish

Development Editors
Pollyanna Poulter and Rachel Morgan

Proofreader
Kate Manson

Indexer
Penny Brown

Illustration
Garry Davies

Icons
Tomek.gr

Series Designers
Shelley Best and Sarah Garbett

Typesetter
Ricky Capanni (International Book Management)

Acknowledgements
Every effort has been made to trace copyright
holders for the works reproduced in this book,
and the publishers apologise for any inadvertent
omissions.

The author would like to thank:
Fieldwork Education (who are responsible for
the International Primary Curriculum) for the
foresight to include enterprise as a core element
within their curriculum and for being available
to answer any questions at a moment's notice.
Particular thanks to Anne Keeling for her energy
and ability to find wonderful case studies at the
drop of a hat.

St Paul's C of E Primary School, Barnet, for
allowing him to try out his enterprise ideas – we
have all benefitted.

His wife, Peachey, and two sons, Sammy and Olly,
who put up with dad getting up at 6am most days
of the summer holiday so that he could get his
latest book written.

About the author
Anthony David is Headteacher of St Paul's C of E
Primary School, London. He is an experienced
author and has written over 60 titles on various
aspects of education.

Contents

Introduction 5

Chapter 1 Money and currency 11

Chapter 2 Shopping 31

Chapter 3 Banking, saving, interest and debt 49

Chapter 4 Ethics and charity 69

Chapter 5 What is enterprise? 89

Chapter 6 Using enterprise 107

Glossary 137

Index 140

Icon key

Information within this book is highlighted in the margins by a series of different icons. They are:

Subject facts
Key subject knowledge is clearly presented and explained in this section.

Why you need to know these facts
Provides justification for understanding the facts that have been explained in the previous section.

Vocabulary
A list of key words, terms and language relevant to the preceding section. Vocabulary entries appear in the glossary.

Amazing facts
Interesting snippets of background knowledge to share.

Common misconceptions
Identifies and corrects some of the common misconceptions and beliefs that may be held about the subject area.

Teaching ideas
Outlines practical teaching suggestions using the knowledge explained in the preceding section.

Golden rules
Core subject concepts which are required to fully understand a subject area.

Questions
Identifies common questions and provides advice on how to answer them.

Handy tips
Specific tips or guidance on best practice in the classroom.

Sensitive issues
Highlights areas that require consideration before presentation to the class, including personal, social and cultural issues.

Financial education

I'm walking through my reception class. Ben stops me: 'Do you want to come to my cafe, Mr David?' he asks. Naturally, I'm delighted. 'What's your cafe called?' I enquire. 'Ben's. Do you want a decaf or skinny? Would you like a biscuit?' It's at this point I'm hit by the depth of role play that I'm being presented with. It's not that he's just pretending to be in a cafe, he is in a *branded* cafe, knows the banter and is trying to up his sale to me! I agree to buy a biscuit.

Children love money. Not because of the 'greed is good' mantra but because it has such an obvious link to the real world. What home corner would be complete without a shop and till? Look at how animated children get when they talk about pocket money, or consider how readily children access money problem-solving questions.

Teenage enterprise can go wrong

Money, finance, enterprise – call it what you will – can be a great tool to teach with. But it can go wrong, as I found out only too well…

It was the early 1980s and computers were just becoming fashionable and affordable. Two friends and I decided an up-to-the-minute computer magazine for pre-teens by pre-teens was needed: *Bit-Mag* was born. We all contributed to writing the magazine, I edited it and one of my friends used his dad's company photocopier to print editions. We agreed to split the profits evenly and all acted as salespeople. Unsurprisingly to us the magazine sold like hot cakes in the playground. We were going to be rich! That was, until we were called to the Headmaster's office. He was furious that we were making money from the school and what he thought was a captive audience by selling an underground magazine about ZX Spectrums. Needless to say, *Bit-Mag* was no more and we were devastated. What is interesting about this story, though, is that we, as three young boys, had shown enterprise and instinctively understood some of the basics of how to run a business by:

- seeing where there was a business opportunity
- recognising and understanding our audience
- working as a team
- delegating roles
- understanding how to use our money
- using our limited budget creatively
- not trying to reinvent the wheel
- being thorough and putting the legwork in.

Importantly we made a profit, albeit a slim and short-lived one. What was wrong was how we went about doing it. Fast forward 30 years and children and young people are still doing the same today. Enterprise is almost instinctive for children, and whether they are attempting to set up an underground magazine or role playing at running a coffee shop in the home corner, children will default to what they understand of the world. The only difference is the level of sophistication. You only have to watch an episode of *Young Apprentice* to see that the 'apprentices' are perfectly mimicking their older counterparts.

A lesson in recent history

The aim of this book is to consider a broad range of strategies that can be implemented across the school to enhance financial understanding. The key question is: Why do we need a book on this subject? Surely the curriculum is crammed enough? Well, time for a short history lesson…

September 2008 is a date that is likely to resound in the annals of history: banks collapsing, respected businesses going into receivership, stock markets crashing and then crashing again, and trillions being wiped off investments. It was an extraordinary period. In a desperate attempt to minimise the effects of recession, the Bank of England on 5 March 2009 practically wiped the idea of an interest rate by reducing it to its lowest level, at 0.5 per cent since the bank was established in 1694. Only Japan had a lower rate (it had been 0.5 per cent since 2001 but was then cut to 0.3 per cent in October 2008). The financial impacts have been swift and acute. The social impacts will, unfortunately, be measured over a longer period of time as the recession hits.

The fundamental question that has been asked is: How did this happen in the first place? After over a decade of growth had we become complacent or was it simply a case of being addicted to debt? Arguably the warning signs had been there for a long time, from the bursting of the digital bubble in the Far East in the early years of the 21st century to the anticipated collapse of an artificially inflated housing market. Had key lessons been ignored? Possibly.

This book also tests the position that schools take on economic well-being. The Every Child Matters (ECM) outcomes (set out in 2004 but then sadly discarded just seven years later) clearly included economic well-being as one of their five core aims. This was reflected in the Cambridge Primary Review (CPR) five years later (*Children, their World, their Education* by Robin Alexander *et al*, Routledge) although neither of these documents was statutory they were strong indicators of how education was evolving. Yet this has been an area that schools have struggled to develop. This is hardly surprising when there is no agreed curriculum to support it. But do schools need an agreed curriculum? In short, no. Way back in 2003, Education Secretary Charles Clarke MP effectively gave schools a licence to develop their own curriculums to meet the needs of their children through the *Excellence and Enjoyment* document. A decade later schools are now taking that licence seriously and developing what they teach, and those that are ahead of the game are making sure that it includes financial education.

Economic well-being will be a key feature of school life if we are to prepare today's children for tomorrow's financial challenges. Inasmuch as a primary school is a forum for teaching children to socially interact it is, equally, an ideal place to teach children how to become financially aware. The social effects of September 2008 will resound in some communities for years. If we're to avoid this happening again we must address the need for economic well-being today. If we don't, we risk failing to prepare children for one of the most significant aspects of their adult life.

How to use this book – what are the short cuts?

So, recent history lesson understood – where does this book fit in and how does it work?

The overall aim of this book is that you should be able to pick it up and gather the necessary information you need to get going with your financial education lesson as soon as possible. Each chapter covers a different area:

● **Chapter 1**: This chapter looks at what money is and provides a brief introduction to how the financial system works. Money is a good way to get children using maths and used to concepts such as decimals.

● **Chapter 2**: Focuses on shopping and how a wide range of shopping experiences can help promote enterprise in the curriculum.

● **Chapter 3**: Looks at the world of banking including savings, interest and debt.

● **Chapter 4**: Explores ethics and charity. Charitable giving (whether financial or time) can be very rewarding and the children should be given opportunities to explore this. They also look at how a small amount of money can be used to make a big difference.

● **Chapter 5**: Looks at what enterprise is and how it relates to education.

● **Chapter 6**: Looks at how to use enterprise in schools.

Teaching is a time-limited profession but if you have time to digest an overview of the book, which you can do by reading the opening pages of each chapter, then I would advise it. This will at least give you a quick understanding of finance from an educational point of view.

In any professional change to education, financial education should be at the forefront. Without it we risk limiting the number of James Dysons or Richard Bransons of the future. Financial education should be fun, dynamic and provide real-time results for children. It's one of the few areas of learning that has an immediate, measurable and understandable impact. If it's that good, surely we should be doing it more often? The aim of this book is to give you licence to integrate realistic and effective financial education into your teaching, bringing together all of the curriculum areas you currently cover into one financially-driven activity focus.

Ben's is open – do you want a biscuit with that?

Money and currency

Money is often the first way into maths for children. It is an immediately practical resource and something that children quickly get their heads round. For example, have you ever noticed that if you present a problem in the form of money children are able to easily handle decimals, percentages, large multiples and multi-stage problems? One reason for this is that money, more than any other mathematical resource, has an immediate impact on everyday life, and many children see adults using it (and therefore modelling its use) frequently. Even in our modern age of online purchasing we still handle cash, and despite some predictions we will do so for many years to come.

History of money

Subject facts

Money is as old as the hills. It is a key element defining a civilised society. Forms of money can be traced back thousands of years. Certainly it had been around for a long time by the time the Mesopotamians came along in about 3000BCE. The British Museum has wonderful artefacts that detail accounting records, which means accountants have been around almost as long as coins.

It is likely that money started with bartering, with livestock or grain being used as a form of currency in the earliest records, around 9000BCE. Livestock and grain are forms of currency that are still used today in parts of Africa. Large-scale projects such as the pyramids of Giza or the Hanging Gardens of Babylon probably would not have been possible without a form of currency and system of money management. Certainly there was a form of currency by 1000BCE, as the Old Testament describes an exchange of gifts between the Queen of Sheba and Solomon that would have included money.

Coinage has taken many forms. In many cultures coins started out in a practical form, and shells were the original coin currency used in China (particularly cowrie shells) around 1200BCE. There is also evidence of shell coinage across Africa and even in the Shetland Islands. The Greeks, taking the lead as they did in many things, take credit for the first types of coin, which Herodotus describes being used in Lydia, in Asia Minor, around 640BCE. These coins were made from electrum, a crude amalgam of gold and silver, which was also used for the first minted coins.

Probably the most famous coin makers were the Romans, who used coins effectively to publicise new leaders of state and emperors. These coins, unlike other currencies, became the first to travel widely internationally; coins of the Emperor Hadrian can be found from Sunderland to Sicily. It was an extremely effective and stable form of currency that was used for hundreds of years and marked the Romans as a stable empire (compare today's euro). The words 'money' and 'mint' are Roman in origin and come from the name for the shrines of Moneta, the goddess of warning. Legend has it that around 390BCE the Gauls attempted to attack the Roman money reserves held in the capital, but nesting geese took flight before they could attack and therefore warned the Roman army, who successfully defended the vaults.

Why you need to know these facts

● Money is central to any civilisation. Understanding its historical use helps define a country. The older the currency, the greater its credibility as it has stood the test of time. It is for this reason that countries or states resist changing currency: it can be interpreted as a sign of instability, which can cause further instability within the country.

● Coins are used to mark historical events, with currency being minted, for instance, for the 2012 London Olympics and a commemorative Diamond Jubilee coin in 2012. Certainly my giving out such coins to children in school was accompanied

by a long speech about how I as a child had been given
a commemorative coin for the Silver Jubilee that I still treasure
today. It is a small piece of history for me, and in the same way
the coin that I was giving each child was a small piece of history
for them. The coin was therefore elevated from necessary
currency tool to historical artefact.

Vocabulary

Coinage – the lowest denominations or parts of a denomination
used within a financial zone.
Currency – the form of money used within a geographic or
financial exchange zone.
Money – a particular form of currency used for financial exchange.

Amazing facts

● The first paper notes appeared in China around 1374CE.

● The Romanian 1 million lei note was issued in 2003, but in
2005 the currency was recalculated and renamed the RON.
1 RON was equivalent to 10,000 lei and so, overnight, the
numbers used on the currency were 10,000 times smaller.

● The world's largest coin was unveiled in Australia on 26
October 2011 to commemorate the Commonwealth Heads of
Government Meeting. It weighs 2,231 pounds, is 31 inches wide,
4.7 inches thick and 99 per cent gold.

● In times of war, coins are often in short supply. Gold and
silver coins are hoarded for their intrinsic value. Other metals
are appropriated for war efforts. Many governments resort to
printing small denomination banknotes as temporary substitutes.
These small denomination bank notes are often small in size.
Some countries that have issued postage stamp sized banknotes
are: Ivory Coast, Macao, Monaco, Morocco, New Caledonia,
Romania, Russia, Spain and the United States.

● The Moroccan 50 centimes 1944 emergency issue, measuring only 43mm by 31mm, is the world's smallest banknote.

Common misconceptions

There is no difference between 'money' and 'currency'.
Money and currency are not one of the same. 'Money' refers to the item that is exchanged for goods, whereas 'currency' is area specific, for example the Venezuelan bolivar or Ugandan shilling.

Teaching ideas

● All currency has great historical value. Historical figures adorn most currencies and that in itself is an interesting avenue for research. Why has this figure been shown? Who are they? Who would you have as your historical figure on the £5 note or £1 coin?

What is money?

Subject facts

The Bank of England used to issue special receipts based on the amount of gold you deposited in the bank. This receipt was trusted as a promise by the bank to pay back the amount of gold deposited and people started to use these notes to pay for things. However, Britain left the 'gold standard' in 1931 so a bank note no longer stands for an amount of gold, but the same trust of notes having a value still exists. Note issue is now backed by securities, not gold.

Currency is a 'promise to pay' for goods. The intrinsic value of a physical paper note is very little, but everyone trusts them and British notes state 'promise to pay' – the note or coin is effectively a glorified 'I owe you.'

Inflation

Rising prices reduces what your money is worth, this is called inflation. The Bank of England set an interest rate to keep inflation low. This influences what people spend and save, and how much things cost.

If inflation is too high (prices are rising too quickly) then the interest rate will be set higher to make saving more attractive and spending less so. If inflation is too low (people are spending less) then the interest rate will be lowered to encourage spending.

Hyperinflation is when there is a very high rate of inflation. It effectively wipes out the purchasing power of private and public savings, which distorts the economy in favour of the hoarding of real assets. This causes the monetary base, the hard currency, to leave the country, and makes the afflicted country an anti-investment zone (something that much of the eurozone is experiencing now). Britain during the 1970s experienced hyperinflation of 25 per cent, but it is generally thought that hyperinflation doesn't begin until a country hits 50 per cent inflation.

Designing money

Notes are made from combinations of historic images, geometric patterns, official currency numbers and watermarks. Designing a currency is not as easy as it looks. The principal historic figure generally appears on the right-hand side of a note and covers about a quarter of it. At the centre of most notes is an empty portrait oval where the watermark sits. Surrounding the image you will often see details of the promissory organisation, such as the Bank of England, the date of issue and the note's value. Good examples are euro notes, and £5 or £10 notes.

Look closely and you will find that complex repeating patterns (called 'Guilloche' patterns) feature on many notes. These provide some forgery security. They are so complex that they are considered almost impossible to replicate without the correct machinery.

What does money represent?

Money is a cycle. We are all familiar with the saying 'Money makes the world go round' but the truth is that it is money which is going round. If you want something, like food or clothing, you need to buy it. In order to buy it you generally need to work for it. If you work for something you need to produce something that can be sold, for someone else to buy. The more popular the item you produce, the more money you can make and therefore the more things you can buy. Value can be identified in practical terms, for example, 'This painting is worth £150', or a virtual value can be assigned, for example Tutor A is judged to be better than Tutor B and therefore can charge a higher rate. Crudely put, money is essentially based on sales, whatever the object that is being sold. In modern times we have managed to rarefy the idea of sales by putting it online (how is Facebook® worth billions?), but at some point somewhere along the line something is being sold. The human philosophy of this is beautifully addressed in Arthur Miller's *Death of a Salesman*.

Money can change

Britain has enjoyed a very stable currency for a long time. Even when it adopted decimalisation in 1971 (see Figure 1 for pre-decimalisation coins) the process was relatively smooth and had few long-term impacts. This is particularly impressive when you consider other states that have attempted similar changes in recent years, in particular the change to using the euro across Europe. This young currency has had a troubled start.

Figure 1 Pre-decimalisation coins

Why you need to know these facts

● It is important to understand that money is the promise of financial value. It is a guarantee that the value printed on the coin or note will be honoured by the bank and then ultimately by the government. If this cannot be assured, either by the bank or the country, then the community will lose confidence in the value of the 'promise' and therefore confidence in money. Without regulation these promises become undermined, which is why so much is invested to ensure that the value of the 'promise' does not collapse.

● When talking about money it is essential to have some. Schools are often awash with plastic coins, which is a good start. However, notes are very useful, particularly £5 notes. As money is not just physical it is also important to obtain examples of cheques and debit or credit cards. For older children it may be useful to show them an online payment system, your school may have its own payment system, such as ParentPay® (which is similar to PayPal™). This would be worth demonstrating as it is likely that a similar system will be the principal form of payment for them in the future.

● Money is often used as a route into learning about decimals. This is a useful way in, however take care when describing the decimal place numbers, as £1.22 said, for example, is often 'one pound twenty-two.' While this adheres to common use of the language it is mathematically incorrect and can lead to children misunderstanding place value. If you are going to use money to introduce decimals it is important to state what the common language practice is (after all, this is what they are going to hear on most occasions) but explain that this is mathematically incorrect and that the numbers refer to tenths and hundredths. It is a small but valuable point to make.

Vocabulary

Guilloche patterns – complex repeating patterns that feature on many notes to prevent fraud.

Hyperinflation – where inflation grossly outweighs the capacity of the currency to keep pace with the price of goods and volume of money generated.

Inflation – a persistent and accumulative rise in general prices related to an increase in volume of money, resulting in a loss of value of the currency.

Sterling – the official economic name for the British currency.

Amazing facts

● Many years ago coins were minted from gold and silver. The pound, when collected in pennies, weighed one pound. The pennies were made from sterling silver. So a pound sterling was equal in value to a pound of sterling silver. Now that coins are made from non-precious metals the name is used to distinguish the British pound from other currencies called pounds.

● Queen Elizabeth II appears on 33 currencies and is the longest reigning head of state to appear on currency – 60 years and counting.

● The note with the highest value currently in circulation, though only used between government agencies, is the American $100,000 Gold Certificate.

● The most expensive note ever sold at auction was the Grand Watermelon, a $1000 American paper note – there are only three in existence. It sold in 2006 for $2,225,000.

Sensitive issues

● Sensitive issues surround money. A friend of mine who worked in the City was happy to announce that he had just received an enormous bonus. When I asked how much that bonus was, I was given a charming but curt reply: 'Dear boy, I couldn't possibly tell you that. Gentleman's code, you know.' Old fashioned as that comment was, it demonstrates that money is not an easy subject to discuss when it gets beyond a certain amount. Principally this is because money clearly defines a social order, particularly for those who see a correlation between money and power. This is clear when you ask children what they get for their pocket money (a subject most children love to talk about). Generally speaking those who think they receive less than others won't be as willing to put their hands up; those who believe they receive an acceptable amount will put their hands up; and then there will be discussions between the groups along the lines 'You get that much?' and 'That's not fair, my parents only give me…' This is hugely revealing, but be aware that a pocket money discussion can be very difficult for some children.

● Money has the power to make or destroy people. This is never clearer than when a family falls into crisis and endures poverty. This has been the case for hundreds of thousands of families over the last few years during the UK's recessionary period. Care must be taken when discussing money. The subject should not be avoided, as it needs to be understood, but if you have children in your class who have free school meals then be mindful when discussing such personal issues.

● Children have a strong moral barometer. As such they will feel uncomfortable if they believe that malpractice is taking place at home. If a child discloses illegal practice to you as a result of a money-based lesson then it should be treated seriously and appropriate steps taken.

Questions

Why is the Queen's head on every coin?
The Queen is the head of our state and it is common in many countries to have the head of state on the currency, a practice popularised by the Romans. All our banknotes bear HM The Queen's head on one side and a famous historical person on the other side.

What is paper money made from?
Different countries use different resources for making paper. In Nigeria, money is printed on a polymer to give it durability. British Sterling is printed on a combination of paper, cotton and linen, with a number of metals interwoven for security reasons. It is relatively fragile and is prone to tears, burns and rips. A study of damaged notes in 2007 revealed:
- 19,788 torn or part notes worth £2,303,000
- 4,748 chewed or eaten notes worth £92,000
- 2,826 washed notes worth £73,000
- 4,295 contaminated notes worth £35,381,000
- 1,454 fire or flood damaged notes worth £2,407,000.

This gave a total of 33,111 damaged notes that together had a total value of £40,256,000.

Why can't we photocopy paper money?
In an attempt to prevent forgery, money is printed on a paper mix that is highly secret. As printing machines become more sophisticated so does money. People have attempted to photocopy money with limited success, and newer photocopiers now have alerts that trigger when money is photocopied. It's not a good idea and can land you in a lot of trouble. Avoid it at all costs.

Why is an MP3 so expensive when you have nothing to hold?
Trade is changing. Increasingly, material goods such as books, films and music are being sold digitally. The reason for this is to increase the efficiency of the sale. A company will make more money if it has fewer overheads, such as paying for a CD case or paper. Equally, it can reach a wider audience more quickly if people can simply download the data. However, with these enormous

economies of scale (the more you produce the cheaper you can produce it) it would be natural to expect that this would impact on the cost of an object, which it hasn't. The question is relevant and one that children should challenge companies with. It raises the question of whether or not companies should pass on their savings to the customer. For example, if a product is cheaper to produce should it be cheaper to buy? Or should a company charge what it believes the customer is willing to pay and make as much profit as it can? This would be a relevant debate to hold in class.

Golden rules

Forgery is illegal. Ensure that the children are very aware of this. If they are making money in school it is only for the purpose of understanding the complex patterns used in its design. Forgery carries a heavy penalty because of the instability that it can potentially create in the economy.

Teaching ideas

● Ask children what they know about money. Ask them to create a mind map and then to share a fact from the map.

● Design your own currency to use in the home corner or a role-play area. Choose a figure that is relevant to your school or area to be on the note and create your own Guilloche pattern using a Spirograph®. You could reduce a Guilloche pattern on a photocopier to make it more intricate.

● Organise the children to work in pairs (both children in a pair need to be from the same year group). Explain that you are interested in finding out which money topics they want to learn more about at school. Give each pair a recording sheet and ask them to consider a range of money topics:
  • ways of getting paid for work
  • how much people earn for different jobs

Money and currency

- what happens if you can't work
- everyday costs of running a house
- ways of paying without cash (coupons or vouchers)
- making decisions about spending
- fair trade
- special offers in shops
- thinking and planning ahead for your money.

Then ask them to think about:

- how much they already know about each topic
- what else they would like to know about each topic.

Some of the money topics may need explaining depending on the age and ability of the children.

● Create a money vocabulary wall. This could form part of a display that the children add to as they work through their money topics.

● Ask small groups to take on the role of a school council and make some decisions about how a budget of £100 should be spent. Explain that the children in their school have made lots of suggestions. As the council they have to spend the money carefully.

Check that all of the children know that a school council is a representative group of children who have been proposed or elected by their peers (other children) to represent their views and raise issues with the senior managers and governors of the school. Being part of a school council is a very important and responsible job: school councils have to represent the views of all the children in the school, even if they don't agree with them.

Work through a series of hypothetical requests (such as better stationery, a class or school pet, better sport resources, investment in an environmental project, a party in celebration of a special event). Give the children a few minutes between each one to discuss their views and make a decision.

Groups should note down each request and predicted cost on a school council budget sheet, and calculate how much of the £100 budget they have spent and how much is left.

At the end, take feedback from the groups to find out which were the most popular choices and why.

● Debate the question: *Is money good?* It is likely that children will have strong feelings about this and will naturally fall into

two camps. Ask the children to group together to make pro-
and anti-money teams. Within these groups ask the children
to break down into groups of around three to discuss reasons
supporting their argument (allow just three minutes – keeping
this discussion tight will encourage sharper answers). At the end
of this session ask if anybody has changed their mind and, if so,
invite them to join another group. Join the small groups together
to create two large groups on opposing sides of the argument.
Give these groups three minutes to share ideas, refine the best
argument and add any new ones; explain they will be presenting
(and therefore arguing) their point to the class in just a few
minutes. Then let the debate begin. It's a fun activity but be careful
to conclude by pointing out the arguments of both groups, and
that the general aim of money is to allow enterprise to operate
smoothly. Do not let the debate go on too long; try and keep the
session tight.

● Discuss the question: *If you borrowed a million pounds, would
you be a millionaire?* Individuals do this all the time but are they
really millionaires? It's an interesting ten-minute discussion.

● *What would you do with £10?* People of all ages would do
different things with different amounts of money. The general
theory is that the smaller the amount, the more likely it is to be
spent on something frivolous. Put this to the test. The children
need to explain their reasons, but try and elicit 'off the top of
their head' ideas rather than giving them too much time to
think about it. Then ask them what they would do with £100,
or £1000, or £1 million. It should become clear that, even among
more confident learners their experience of money is limited
to below £100. Most children are unaware of the true value of
expensive items such as cars, holidays and houses.

● Discuss how money makes us feel. It can make us feel excited,
disappointed, motivated and jealous, sometimes all at once. We
need to understand how money makes us feel so we can manage
our emotions. Discuss the following about feeling sad and happy
about money – do the children think this is always true?
We feel sad when we:
  • only have a small amount of money
  • don't have enough money

- are in debt (this will be discussed later in the book)
- pay all the bills and don't have much money left
- lose money.

We feel happy when we:
- have lots of money and are rich
- win at Bingo
- have extra money to save
- find a bargain
- give to charity
- have more money than our friends or family
- have enough money to do what we want with it
- buy something we really like or need.

● Put an image of a jar of coins on a money display board and leave it there for children to think about. Does anyone have something like this at home? Is it ever used? What is its purpose? Change the picture to a homeless person. How does this image make the children feel? Invite children to introduce their own money-related stimulus pictures for the board.

● Display a range of items on a table, for example a bottle of water, a toilet roll, a sparkly necklace, an apple, a holiday brochure, a t-shirt and a mobile phone. Ask the children to divide these items into 'needs' and 'wants'. Certain items will create great discussion, particularly the mobile phone.
- 'Needs' are items that are essential to health and well-being, such as food, clothing and shelter.
- 'Wants' are non-essential items, sometimes called luxuries, such as jewellery.

Explain to the children that they need to give younger children advice about why they should spend their money on 'needs' before 'wants'. Their advice could be written in sentences that start with *What I really, really want is X but what I really need is X because…*

● Pocket money can be a great way to teach children money management skills and help them learn how to make decisions, deal with limited resources, and understand the benefits of saving and charitable giving. There's no single correct way to handle giving pocket money. Deciding when to start, how much to give, and whether you want to link the allowance to chores are choices that should fit each family. Ask the children what they think is a fair amount of pocket money (this will take individuals out of the equation and therefore reduce the 'pecking order' issues surrounding this subject) and when they should start to earn pocket money. Then ask the children how they should receive the money, should it be given or linked to an activity such as tidying their bedroom or putting out rubbish? If it is linked to an activity should it be given each time the activity is done (payment on work done) or as a given sum at the end of the week (like a wage or salary)? This will open up a debate and seed the idea that money is generally given for a service or commodity.

● Put children in the role of 'Agony Aunt' and pose them a money-related problem, for example 'I've just found £5 on the floor, what should I do?'

● Children's money personalities will determine how they handle their money. 'Spenders' spend first and ask questions later. 'Savers' ask questions and find a reason not to spend. No matter what their personality, as long as you are aware of it, you can help them make the appropriate adjustments. It is necessary that we spend for a healthy economy, but we also need to save to make it through the 'down' cycles. Children tend to be spenders as most do not have to account for the money they have spent, but it is useful to make them aware of the different perspectives.

● Money is a great way to introduce children to decimals, as it means they regularly see numbers presented to two decimal places. Use a range of priced goods, and ask the children to convert the amounts from pounds into pence.

Money around the world

Subject facts

Currency, next to its flag, is often what defines a country. The US dollar is a universally recognised note and is as American as Uncle Sam. The same could be said about many of the former European currencies, such as the French franc, Italian lira or Spanish peseta. The euro has been in circulation across Europe since 1999 so you may well find that children are unaware of and unfamiliar with a number of the former European currencies.

Currency exchange

Currency exchange is essentially to change one type of currency into another. Exchange rates change daily based on economic factors. The exchange rate given tells you how much of your currency you will get in another, for example £1 might be worth $2 if the exchange rate was 2.0 (two times as much). Typically, the exchange rate is not an exact figure, it often contains many decimal points.

Something to think about

Children understand the basics of finance and therefore the impacts of illegal practices such as theft. The theft of money was once relatively rare: to steal money was a relatively high risk, bold act with the chance of very little return and a heavy penalty if caught (which is more likely than for most other forms of crime as generally there will be witnesses or some form of CCTV at a money source). However, with online retail booming so is online theft. Unlike its old-fashioned relative, online theft is relatively low risk (very few get caught) with high returns, often worth several thousand pounds. It is also a growing problem: historically it would have been unlikely that you would have met anybody who had had their money stolen whereas most staffrooms will have at least one member of staff who has lost money via an online transaction. This is a valid opportunity to reinforce good e-safety practices with children, for example when inputting personal details on a website.

Why you need to know these facts

- Given the extraordinarily international make-up of the UK, currency offers a clear route into celebrating a child's heritage in a meaningful way.

- Children understand more about money than we generally give them credit for. As I mentioned at the start of this chapter, if a mathematical problem is presented as a money problem children generally find it easier to understand (take, for example, multiplying with £5 or introducing decimals with pounds and pence).

● It is highly likely that children in your class will visit either Europe or America. As a result it is important that they understand the currency exchange rates for these two financial zones. What might seem expensive because it has a higher number in the local currency unit than it does in the UK may, once exchanged, turn out to be a similar price. Understanding how to exchange money is important if children are to be able to gauge the value of an item against commonly understood monetary value (in our case, pounds sterling).

Vocabulary

Currency exchange – to change one type of currency into another.

Amazing facts

● In 1988, to commemorate the centenary of independence from more than 300 years of Spanish colonial rule, the government of the Philippines issued the world's largest banknote, measuring 355.6mm by 215.9mm. This beat the previous record set by the Chinese Ming Dynasty 1 kuan, which measured 220mm by 335mm.

● The note with the most zeros on it is the Zimbabwean 100 trillion (100,000,000,000,000) dollar note (issued in 2009). The note has 14 zeros printed on both the front and the back.

● There are over 60 communities throughout the United States that have their own form of local currency. Some of the more popular are in Ithaca in New York, Berkshire in Massachusetts and Walt Disney World theme park. California has the most

communities with their own currency, including many colleges
such as Berkeley and Santa Barbara, also George Lucas' Skywalker
Ranch, where his various cinema-related businesses operate.

- The widely known $ sign does not appear on any US notes.

Sensitive issues

Currencies change, particularly when there is significant political
change or geographic realignment (where borders are redrawn
generally as a result of conflict). The previous currency is then
a powerful symbol of an old regime. Care should be taken when
discussing historic currencies, particularly recent ones, that you
don't inadvertently offend a child or their family.

Teaching ideas

- A simple but enduring idea is to create a currency world map.
Pin a large map to your money display and invite children to
add to it with local currencies that they may have left over from
foreign holidays. If possible, ask children to bring in notes and
coins, as they are generally quite different. This is an opportunity
for families to search out their old European currency, some of
which may now be relatively worthless (a good illustration of the
fact that currency is merely a 'promise' of worth). Once collected,
analyse the different currencies. They will be made from different
materials (for example, Australian currency feels as if it's made
from plastic in order to keep it durable and less likely to tear
in the wash) and will certainly have different images on them.
Also the patterns and images used will differ widely. If possible,
either provide children with magnifying glasses or connect
a digital magnifier to your interactive whiteboard. This will
give children the opportunity to analyse the notes. Ask the
children: *Who is Andrew Bailey (his name is found on £10 notes)?
Which countries use the euro?*

Most countries use a watermark on their notes as part
of their forgery defence. The watermark on Commonwealth

notes is generally the Queen, as head of state. Who is used for other watermarks?

● Ask the children what design they would put on a coin, if they could, and why. Can they design a personal currency and what would its value be? Which historical figure would they put on their notes and why? Ask them to ask their families.

● Create a simple currency exchange between sterling (£) and a currency for your school, say, 'le school-o' (S). When at school the children need to work out how much their meal will cost in sterling, given school-o prices, for example:

Starters	Mains	Desserts
Bread S3	Pizza S10	Chocolate melt S6
Olives S4	Pasta S8	Strawberry cupcake S4
Garlic bread S5	Salad S9	Banana float S5

Adapt the activity by adjusting the currency exchange rate, for example S3 for every £1 or S1.50 for every £1.

Resources

Websites
Personal Finance Education Group (PFEG): www.pfeg.org
Bank of England: www.bankofengland.co.uk
The Treasury: www.hm-treasury.gov.uk

Books
The Pocket Money Plan: A Practical Guide to Teaching Your Children about Money by Julie Hedge (Ovolo Books).
Death of a Salesman by Arthur Miller (Viking Press).

Shopping

Shopping is something that many of us enjoy, whether it is flicking through a catalogue, surfing the net for a bargain, trawling the high street, or simply the weekly food shop. Shopping is something that, as a country, we spend hours doing every week and spend billions of pounds of our hard-earned money on. It is also something that children understand, as generally, they are shadowing their parents in these various shopping locations. As a result it is an area of learning that children feel they can role play with confidence.

This chapter will consider how a wide range of shopping experiences can help promote enterprise in the curriculum from the foundation stage through to Year 6 and beyond.

Where to shop

Subject facts

Shopping is something that has changed considerably over the last few years. High streets have always been evolving centres but have undergone a dramatic change in the last decade with the growth of out-of-city hypermarkets and the long-term impacts of the recession. Online shopping has also dramatically changed the way we shop; this is reflected by the number of empty shops on the high street.

A shop is an ideal situation for home corners. The home corner promotes dramatic play, both for individual children and for children participating in cooperative play. It is an area that you can adapt for all kinds of role play. Most nurseries and Reception classes have a home corner where young children are encouraged to play 'house'. Give the children things that they see in their home and they will mimic what they have seen adults doing.

Shops

Maths comes alive when it has a real-life source. The corner shop provides a great location for small money problems. It is somewhere that children generally know and it is likely that your school has a corner shop near it.

Equally, supermarkets are somewhere that children are likely to have a great deal of familiarity with. These environments also produce large amounts of data in the form of till receipts which can be a useful resource when teaching.

Cafes and restaurants

As illustrated in the Introduction by the example of Ben's cafe, places where you eat are familiar territory for children. The high street has changed from a product-led to a service-led centre as a result of the recession driving out the likes of Woolworths and MFI and replacing them with cafes and restaurants.

This also reflects the change in how consumers are spending their money: like our American cousins, we are increasingly dining out. It stands to reason that children are not only comfortable in these settings but also understand them well.

Why you need to know these facts

- Using familiar situations, such as shops, provides a real-world context for children to use money and make transactions.

- Using the corner shop theme is a great way to pitch some standard money problems based around pocket money amounts.

Vocabulary

Product – something made or created, generally for sale.
Shop – a retail business selling a product or service.

Amazing facts

● Chiddingstone Stores and Post Office in Kent is England's oldest shop. It dates back to 1593, making it more than 500 years old.

● The Little Espresso Co. in Lincoln is England's smallest cafe. At 2 metres square it can hold just two people sitting at the bar and two in the queue.

● Starbucks is the world's most popular coffeehouse. In less than 25 years it has managed to open nearly 20,000 cafes in nearly 60 countries around the world. However, this is small when compared to the giant fast food chain McDonald's, which operates in 119 countries worldwide, owns over 31,000 restaurants, serves 58 million people daily and employs approximately 1.5 million people.

Sensitive issues

Never assume that all children's home backgrounds are the same. Be aware of financial and cultural differences. Remember that there will be a huge difference in the way that families prioritise, value and access money, regardless of culture or financial background. Whenever discussing money, particularly if it falls into the realms of pocket money, children can be tempted to 'showboat'. Sometimes amounts can be wildly exaggerated but whether exaggerated or true they can cause discomfort in the class and establish an unnecessary hierarchy.

Lessons can be supported by some simple ground rules, such as:
- taking turns, listening carefully and respecting comments
- ensuring that lessons are general in content and therefore there is little opportunity to personalise them
- providing opportunities for small group or paired discussions, which are generally less threatening than whole-class ones.

Teaching ideas

● If you have a local shop, take a photograph (ask the proprietor's permission) and use it to give money problems a real-world feel (although it is unlikely that the proprietor would mind it is always best to ask permission first). Use it to answer questions such as:

- I had 20 pence. I bought a book for 12 pence. How much money do I have left?
- I had 38 pence. I dropped 15 pence. How much money do I have left? Draw the coins I might have.
- I had 18 pence. My mum gave me 3 pence more. How much do I have altogether?
- I had 76 pence. I bought a book for 4 pence and a bag of sweets for 12 pence. How much do I have left? Show at least two different ways of making the amount you have left with coins.
- I had 87 pence. I bought a cake for 22 pence and a chocolate bar for 9 pence. How much do I have left? Show at least two different ways of making the amount you have left with coins.
- I had 55 pence. Mum gave me a 10 pence coin, a 5 pence coin and a 2 pence coin. How much do I have altogether? Show at least two different ways of making this amount with coins.

These examples can be edited by changing the values to create more or less sophisticated versions of the same question. They are always best supported by using real coins, particularly with younger year groups.

● Receipts offer scope for many questions that can be used to open a lesson. You will obviously need to tailor these to match the receipt but some examples are:

- How many items did I buy?
- What was the most expensive item on the receipt?
- How much was spent in total?
- I bought two baguettes. How much would one baguette cost?
- I bought 500g of grapes. How much would 1kg cost? What would 3kg cost? What would 250g cost?
- Calculate how much two bunches of flowers would cost.

- If I hadn't bought the baguettes how much would the bill be?
- What change would I get from a £20 note?
- If I had bought a magazine at the till that cost £3.95 what would the new total be? Would I need more or less than £20 to pay it?

These are questions that start children investigating the price of products.

● The home corner is most useful in helping children with their social and language skills, which can be wonderfully complex and sophisticated if they are given a real-life setting and if that setting is regularly changed (at least once every half term). Below are a list of suggested themes for different home corners that will help draw out different forms of language and maths:

- cafe
- garden centre
- airport
- bakery
- restaurant
- toy shop
- train station
- supermarket.

Things that children can do in a themed home corner include:

- counting out coins to pay the shopkeeper or ticket collector
- writing menus and price lists
- making travel tickets, showing the price and the seat number
- making price labels and sticking them on goods
- weighing luggage on bathroom scales
- arranging seats to create a train, coach or plane and numbering each one.

Logic questions that could be used in a bakery or supermarket home corner could include:

- How many X are there?
- Which carrier bag holds the most items?
- Should the bigger items cost more, less or the same?

● Larger sums of money require the same strategy for addition as decimal numbers. Choose two items from the board. Items can vary but for Year 3 they could consist of, for example: toy car £1.75; castle £5.30; doll £3.25; construction set £7.20; animal collection £1.95.

Explain that the children are going to group the numbers into pounds and pence and add them. For example the cost of a construction set and toy car would be explained as:

Construction set and toy car:	£7.20 + £1.75
Construction set:	£7 + £0.20 = £7.20
Toy car:	£1 + £0.75 = £1.75
Adding pounds:	£7 + £1 = £8
Adding pence:	£0.75 + £0.20 = £0.95
Adding it all together:	£8 + £0.95 = £8.95

Ask the children to try combinations of products. They can create multiple pairs, such as two toy cars, or add more than two items. The main idea is to encourage them to see that adding the largest element of the number first will help them to gain a reasonable idea of what the final total will be. This will help them to assess their final results themselves – if they found that the total for the construction set and toy car was £12.65 they should immediately want to review their figures, understanding that £7 + £1 = £8 and therefore that £12.65 is significantly higher and unlikely to be correct.

● Use a cafe theme to teach simple maths ideas and introduce tasks such as:
  • Round items on a receipt to the nearest tenth or pound.
  • Give the right change. Calculate how much change will be given if you buy a hot chocolate and a cake with £5, £10 or £20. (Use real-life examples of prices.)
  • Use chunking skills to multiply and find the price of three coffees and two cakes.

● Ask the children to discuss what they expect to find on a restaurant menu and record their responses. Ask groups to look at example menus you have supplied. They should review them and add any further features to the list. Discuss the key elements together and discuss differences between the type of restaurants and the type of customers. Create a set of rules for a class menu.

● Ask the children to consider kinds of restaurants that they might write their own menus for. They could look at additional sample menus, cookbooks and other resources on the particular kind of food or restaurant they have chosen.

● Ask the children to create menus individually or in a group. Plan the menu by asking them to note down what they want to include (for example, specific food items, restaurant details, or special offers) they should also consider the audience for their restaurant. Then they should draft their menus, including price details before preparing a finalised version.

Markets

Subject facts

Markets have been around for millennia and are possibly the oldest form of trading. Almost every form of civilisation or social group will have its version of a market. The forms of market that are described in this book are traditional English markets – the car boot sale and farmers' market – but a market in Uganda will be as radically different to an English farmers' market as a Moroccan souk is to the Newcastle dockside market.

Markets can often reflect the personality of a community and are important centres of commerce. As a result they are a powerful way to engage with the various communities represented in your school by discussing and sharing experiences of marketplaces. Wherever the community comes from, markets are always busy and loud places with everybody trying to get a good bargain. Farmers' markets are a common site in many places around the UK.

Why you need to know these facts

● There are a wide range of skills that can be taught at markets, including risk and assessing a product's value: have you got something that is value for money or not? It is worth discussing the following questions:
- How can you negotiate?
- What tactics can you use?
- What is haggling and what do you expect the outcome to be?
- What are the risks involved?

Vocabulary

Market – a communal gathering place for buying or selling; can be a collection of stalls or shops.

Teaching ideas

● Find out if there is a local farmers' market that you could investigate as a class. Discuss the financial benefits, if any, of buying directly from the supplier. You could visit it and carry out a survey in your local town to see who uses the farmers' market and what is on sale.

● Create a role play of haggling, as if at a car boot sale, in the class.

● 'Pick-your-own' farms allow you to choose the fruit and vegetables and pick very fresh food straight from the ground, in season. Have any of the children been to a pick-your-own farm? How did they find it? What do they think the advantages and disadvantages are of picking your own food? Ask the children to talk about the financial implications with a partner.

● Discuss what advantages there might be for farmers and growers in selling direct to the public. How can it help their businesses?

● Model using the £ sign and decimal places correctly. For example £6.20 for 'six pounds twenty', not £6.2.

● Model using a calculator to work through this multi-step problem: Can you find ½ of £2.40 and 30 per cent of £3? If these were sale prices how much have you spent? How much have you saved?

● Model working out how much 50g of apples would cost at £1.50 per kilo, then how much 25g of apples would cost.

● Think of some word problems related to which fruit or vegetable is the most or least expensive per 25g, 50g, 1kg, where the price is £2 per kilogram.

- Apply this method to word problems involving volumes of liquids.
- Repeat with different figures asking for volunteers to complete each step of the problem.

Online shopping

Subject facts

The internet came of age as an economic force in the recession of 2008–10. The importance of the internet to the daily lives of consumers, of all age groups, has become deeper and more valued. Among other things, people use the internet to search for new and innovative ways to make their money go further, to look for jobs, and to buy and sell second-hand items. To an increasing extent the internet is becoming an integral, arguably vital, medium for social engagement. It has effectively become a key life-management tool, and it will become ever more important in the new 'age of austerity'. Generally when people buy online it is to save money. It is far easier to compare products online than it is in shops and, generally speaking, savings are greater.

In schools our temptation is to be overly safety conscious and therefore restrictive of internet use. While there are very good reasons for this, Becta in its e-safety report gave schools fair warning, quoting in turn a report from the think tank Demos, which found that digital technology has become fully integrated into children's daily lives:

> *Undoubtedly new technologies bring new risks, but the Demos authors found that 'contrary to society's assumptions about safety, this generation is also capable of self-regulation when kept well-informed about levels of risk'. Schools have a duty to help children and young people remain safe when online, whether that use of the internet occurs inside or outside school. Also, as the Demos report states, 'schools need to respond to the way young people are learning outside the classroom' and 'develop strategies to bridge formal and informal learning, home and school'.*
>
> Signposts to Safety (Becta, 2007)

Why you need to know these facts

● Today's generation are being brought up in a culture where online shopping sits side by side with high-street shopping. Indeed, they may be more familiar with the online version and therefore more savvy to its potential risks.

● Online shopping happens at home whether it is in the form of casual music downloads, or purchase of virtual or physical items. Money online has a different 'feel' and many organisations make it very easy for users to purchase items. Children therefore need to understand the impact of the cost of an item, virtual or physical, in a way that is very different to just a few years ago. It is this form of technology, which schools have barely begun to address, that could be most critical for children in their futures.

Amazing facts

● Amazon™ found that when it started offering digital versions of its books, book sales changed completely. Rather than people buying books during the day they were buying them late in the evening. The conclusion was that when somebody had finished a book they wanted a new one immediately. Digital books offer that option and, as a result, sales reflected instant demand.

● The first online retailer was Pizza Hut, which started offering pizza online in 1994.

Teaching ideas

● Questions to consider about buying online are:
  • Have you or your parents ever bought something online?
  • What types of things do people generally tend to buy online?
  • Why would you buy online?
  • Have you ever been surprised by what you've received?

- Has someone you know ever made a mistake?
- What wouldn't you buy online or what can't you buy online (a haircut for example)?
- Where do you do most of your shopping?

Shopping trends and environmental impacts

Subject facts

For a number of years following the Second World War most shopping was still done locally. There were not the big out-of-town centres that we have now; people purchased their groceries in the small, local shops on the high street. In addition, many foods were only available when they were in season.

Packaging

Post-war shoppers did not help themselves to the goods in shops, items were picked and weighed for them by assistants. There was much less packaging and so not as much waste as there is today, and there was no recycling of packaging. The goods were put in paper bags or went straight into shopping baskets. One of the main differences for today's shopper is the plastic bags given out by many shops or taken to the shops by the shopper.

The plastic bags that we use nowadays cause problems in landfill sites. This is because many of them are not biodegradable and therefore do not break down. Also, plastic bags are often thrown away, making the countryside look untidy as well as being a danger to animals.

Several shops have started charging for carrier bags in an effort to reduce the number consumers use and in Wales a 5p fee applies to every carrier bag.

A global marketplace

Consumers like to be able to buy produce from supermarkets all year round, even when it is not in season in Britain, so they can eat their favourite foods and have a wide variety of menus.

Although many raw materials come from less economically developed countries in the South, they are often manufactured in Britain or other northern countries. The original product looks quite different from the manufactured goods we buy in our supermarkets. This expensive packaging results in, among other things, high retail prices.

Fair trade

What is it? Fair trade is described by the Fairtrade Foundation as:

> *A strategy for poverty alleviation and sustainable development. Its purpose is to create opportunities for producers and workers who have been economically disadvantaged or marginalized by the conventional trading system. If fair access to markets under better trade conditions would help them to overcome barriers to development, they can join Fairtrade.*

Fair trade has been around for many years and certainly over the last decade public awareness of it has grown in much the same way as awareness of organic farming. Today many products carry the FAIRTRADE Mark, including sugar, tea, coffee and bananas. In some supermarkets some products such as bananas have become exclusively fair trade. When you see the Mark on products it means that farmers in developing countries have been paid a fair and stable price as well as the Fairtrade premium, an additional sum of money which they choose how to invest in their communities. When you see the Mark on cotton it relates to the cotton farmers, not the whole manufacturing process.

Figure 2 Fairtrade logo

Sweatshops

Sweatshops are factories where products are made by underage, significantly underpaid people. They can be found all over the world. Certainly as the economy shrinks the likelihood of these factories being used intensifies. Clothes are particularly likely to have been made using sweatshop labour. The facts are shocking and the exploitation of women in particular is horrifying. While hard facts are very difficult to obtain it is believed that:

- 85 per cent of sweatshop workers are young women between the ages of 15 and 25.
- Sweatshop workers earn as little as a quarter to half of what they need for basic nutrition, shelter, energy, clothing, education and transportation.
- In order to meet the basic nutritional needs of their families, sweatshop workers spend between 50 and 75 per cent of their income on food alone.
- Almost 75 per cent of the retail price of a garment is pure profit for the manufacturer and retailer.
- While the garment industry is notorious for its involvement in the sweatshop industry, it is not the only culprit. Common sweatshop goods include tyres, auto parts, shoes, toys, computer parts and electronics.
- There are probably sweatshops in every country in the world – anywhere where there is a pool of desperate, exploitable workers. Logically, the poorer the country, the more exploitable its people are. Labour violations are therefore especially widespread in less economically developed countries.

Why you need to know these facts

● Consumers often do not think about the origin of the food they buy in the supermarket but it is important to discuss the effect that this has on communities and the environment, both locally and globally.

Vocabulary

Sweatshop – a factory where forced labour is used to create products.

Amazing facts

● The estimated retail value of Fairtrade coffee rose from £18.6 million in 2001 to £194.3 million in 2011. Sugar has seen even greater growth, from £4.5 million in 2001 to £464.1 million in 2011. Chocolate is listed separately as it is a mix of cocoa and sugar. However, the rise in Fairtrade chocolate is impressive – over the same period it rose in value from £5.4 million to £413.1 million.

Teaching ideas

● Visit a local supermarket. Select some products and see what the children can find out about them from the packaging. Can they find the product's country of origin? Back in the classroom, ask them to locate the countries on a map or in an atlas and discuss how long it might have taken to get the produce to the UK. Calculate the food miles (the distance travelled).

● Ask the children to consider some of the arguments for having seasonal food available all year round, for example:
  • to keep people in work in countries such as Kenya, allowing them the opportunity to make enough money to feed their families
  • to keep a variety of foods available for customers.
Discuss why people may have concerns about this way of shopping and why the desire to bridge the gap between consumers and producers has been growing. Many measures have been put in place in an attempt to reconnect people with farming and the origins of their food. Research some of these.

● Have some shopping bags and plastic bags available to show the children. Ask them why they think plastic bags are so popular. Ideas may include: cost; ease of storage when empty; bright and colourful designs; and the advertising slogans visible to other shoppers.

● Ask the children what sort of food shops they think would have been found on a typical post-war high street (grocers, greengrocers, butchers, bakers and so on). Show them a picture of an old shop front that you can use as focus for the discussion. If you are studying a particular period in history then use an image from that time. Do shops like that still exist in the neighbourhood of your school?

● Look into organisations that are keen to support British or local foods and discuss why this may be.

● Are there any speciality foods produced and/or available locally in your area? Look in local directories or newspapers, also see: www.localfoodadvisor.com

● Provide a selection of goods that were grown overseas, for example: rice, sugar, cotton wool, tea, flowers, bananas, coffee, oranges, orange juice, chocolate, sweetcorn, tinned fruit. Display them and discuss the following points:
  • Where do the children think these items originally came from?
  • Is this the same as where they were made or manufactured? (Look it up on the package if the children are unsure.)
  • Do the children know where this country is?
Ask the children to find out three further facts about the items on the table or the countries where the products were grown. Do all of the items come from countries south of the equator? Which of the items come from more than one country? Ask the children to find other countries where these items come from. Many of the items consumed in Britain, or in other northern countries, come from raw materials imported from countries in the South.

● Review the meaning of 'fair trade' with the class. What is it? What's the Fairtrade premium and how does it help producer groups in the developing world? What does it mean to them? What would make the children buy or convince their parents to buy fair trade goods? What are the arguments against fair trade? Give groups one of the following fair trade products:

- raisins
- honey
- blueberries
- sugar
- rice.

The children should discuss their products, to create product profiles, focusing on questions such as:

- What does it look like?
- Where does it come from?
- How is it grown?

Groups then use their profiles to discover five facts about their product to share with the class.

● Role play a world fair trade marketplace where different producer groups try to persuade shoppers in the UK to buy their fair trade products. Using their knowledge about their product, they need to develop a convincing argument, which they will then present to the class. Share ideas for what makes a good argument.

● Bring in a piece of sugar cane or sugar beet or use an image of one. Ask the children if they know what food item this is, or what food is made from this.

● Introduce photos of raw materials such as coffee beans, sugar cane and cocoa pods, and some manufactured products made from them. Are there any materials or products that the class are unsure about? What do they think they could be? Ask the children to discuss the following questions: *What are the similarities and differences between raw materials and their manufactured products? Why is this? What happens with the products? How does the raw material change? Does it change shape and colour? Do you think it is cooked, heated, cooled, refrigerated, mashed, cubed…?* Explore the sugar supply chain with the class and compare it with the children's answers to the questions.

● Divide the children into small groups. Each group chooses a product (tea, coffee, cocoa) and tries to find as much information as possible about its supply chain. They can share their findings and create a display, painting or newspaper article.

● Collect a variety of different types of packaging (preferably showing retail prices). Ask the children to examine whether certain materials used for packaging have an impact on the cost of an item. They could record some of their findings in a simple table.

Resources

Useful websites
Fair trade:
www.fairtrade.org.uk
www.wfto.com
www.traidcraftshop.co.uk

Farmers' markets:
www.localfoods.org.uk
www.farma.org.uk/
www.lfm.org.uk (for the London area)

Sweatshops:
www.dosomething.org

Food:
www.redtractor.org.uk
www.organiclinker.com/food-miles.cfm
www.localfoodadvisor.com

Reports
Signposts to Safety: Teaching E-Safety at Key Stages 3 and 4 by Becta (Becta, 2007).

Books
Sustainable Food: A No-fluff Guide to Farmers Markets And Eating Locally by James Rockwell (Simple Self-sufficiency).
Farmers' Market edited by Jesse Russell and Ronald Cohn (Books on Demand Ltd).
The Fair Trade Revolution edited by John Bowes (Pluto Press).
50 Reasons to Buy Fair Trade by Miles Litvinoff and John Madeley (Pluto Press).

Banking, saving, interest and debt

It is common for the children to visit banks with their families and see actions taking place that involve money. Typically there are three aspects to this: spending, saving and investing. Increasingly banking is moving online, but the subject facts remain the same. In class, banking is a great model for any number of maths activities, but particularly calculation.

Banking

Subject facts

Banking dates far back into history and indeed forms an important aspect of classical studies, as many of the first records kept were accounts. The history of banking begins with the proto-banks run by merchants of the ancient world, which made grain loans to farmers and traders who carried goods between cities. This began around 2000BCE in Assyria and Babylonia. Later, in ancient Greece and during the Roman Empire, lenders based in temples made loans and added two important innovations: they accepted deposits and changed money. Archaeology from this period in China and India also shows evidence of moneylending activity.

The oldest bank in the world is the Banca Monte dei Paschi di Siena, Italy. Originally formed as the Monte di Pietà or Monte Pio in 1472, it made loans to the poor out of charity. *Monte*, meaning 'heap' or 'pile', referred to the collection of money used for charitable distribution, and the bank truly served to benefit the city's economy. The word 'bank' is from the Italian *banca*, meaning a bench or counter.

The Bank of England was founded by William Paterson after King William III of England found himself badly in need of funds to fight a war with France in 1694. Paterson provided the funds after the king agreed to order all the goldsmiths of London to stop issuing receipts as depositories for precious metals, forcing merchants to store their gold with the new bank. The Bank of England was finally nationalised in 1946 and acts as the central bank for the UK, setting monetary policy for the country.

Today, banking is a part of everyday life. Most people will have some type of bank account, where the bank agrees to hold funds for a customer under their name and with a unique account number. Banks secure people's funds and track transactions. Almost every business, charity, school and home will have a bank account. These need to be checked and money must be followed so that the value of the money remains accurate and that no single account holder is receiving more or less than they should. Statements are a cross-reference checking document for money that has gone in and out of the account. An internet search of 'example bank statements' will provide you with examples to use in class. When an account is overspent (and a consumer is using an overdraft, meaning they have drawn out funds beyond £0) it is sometimes referred to as being 'in the red'. In some cases the balance will be printed in red to alert the account holder that they are currently overdrawn.

Statements are, effectively, a multi-step money problem involving addition, subtraction and cross-referencing for checking. Checking a statement is important as banks can make mistakes, particularly if they are managing millions of customers' accounts, each with hundreds of bank transactions every month (each time they pay a bill, receive a salary statement, do the food shopping and so on).

The arrival of the internet and the growing usage of personal computers presented a great opportunity for the banking industry to transform the way people conduct their banking. Experimentation with online banking started during the early 1980s, but it wasn't until 6 October 1995 that Presidential Savings Bank first offered customers an online alternative to the traditional banking experience. Soon after, Wells Fargo, Chase Manhattan and Security First National Bank offered online banking, too. The early days were challenging and reports of banks losing account holders' details quickly hit the news, but nearly 20 years later security systems have greatly improved and online banking is an everyday tool for millions of people.

Why you need to know these facts

● Given the global impact of the financial crisis, particularly within the eurozone, it is unlikely that banks will leave the headlines soon. Even when times are good they are often in the spotlight simply because they impact on our everyday lives.

● It's important to understand the purpose of banks and why they exist. Ask the children if they have anything precious and, if so, where they keep it and how they would feel if it got lost.

Vocabulary

Account – an agreement between the bank and the customer for the holding of funds. An account is stored along with the person's name and unique account number.

Account number – this is a unique number that identifies the account details of the banking customer. It is a very private number that should be known only to the owner of the money in the account.

Balance – this is the total amount of money you have in your account.

Statement – this is where you keep track of how much money has been added and subtracted from your bank account on paper. You add what you deposit and subtract what you spend.

Amazing facts

● The Bank of America is, unsurprisingly, the richest bank in the world, and is worth around £162 billion (as of 2012). Indeed, three out of the five richest banks are American, though there are a growing number of very rich Asian banks.

● The biggest bank robbery in British history took place on 21 February 2006 in Kent. Six robbers managed to steal over £53 million from the cash deposit at the Securitas depot. The Securitas heist was unique and by far the largest 'real' robbery, however it is believed that over £1 billion is stolen every year in virtual theft through online banking or sales, a figure equivalent to a Securitas heist twice a month.

Sensitive issues

It is unlikely that you will be aware of the financial situations of your children's families. When discussing credit, loans or other banking subjects be sensitive about the impacts of financial errors. For some families debt (which is covered later in this chapter) is a result of irresponsibility. But for many more debt has occurred as a result of failing to be able to meet the bills. The impact of not being able to access money or, worse still, seeing a future with less money available, has a global impact on families no matter how wealthy they may be.

Common misconceptions

● There are many common misconceptions about banks and money (the two are intrinsically linked). Myths such as money making you happy, big incomes keeping you out of debt, money finding love, money finding friends, money providing fun are generally speaking untrue. A damaging misconception about banks is that they don't care about you and are trying to steal your money. This is not the case and in many ways banks would rather go out of their way to make you feel that your money is secure with them. Failure to do this risks loss of trust. Any hint of loss of trust will have an immediate impact on the stock exchange (the exchange is not a clinical institution and is sensitive to uncertainty), which can, in extreme cases, cause a run on the banks. This happened in 2007 to Northern Rock – the first bank run in the UK in over 100 years. In general, banks want to work with you – they're not as bad as they're made out to be!

● Never assume children understand what a bank is. Children's exposure to money is limited and often their understanding of what a bank does is equally limited.

Handy tip

Many banks are prepared to send staff to nearby schools to talk to children (indeed many banks run schemes where employees regularly visit schools to support activities such as reading or maths). Bringing in a guest speaker brings an activity alive and is well worth the extra effort.

Teaching ideas

● Discuss with the children what they think banks do and what they are for. Provide an example statement and ask the children to look at it and discuss what the various columns mean. Typically there are five columns on a bank statement:

- date
- transaction details (sometimes split into two columns: reference number and title)
- debit
- credit
- balance.

Explain to the children that generally the credit column will be more than the debit column, as that means you have more money going into your account than you are spending.

● Discuss some moral dilemmas and practical questions, for example:
- What should you do if you find your account has too much money in it because of an obvious banking error?
- What should you do if you discover somebody else has used your account for an online transaction?

Saving

Subject facts

Savings typically fall into three brackets:
- current
- short-term
- medium- or long-term.

Most adults have a current account, that is used to hold their general day-to-day funds for utilities, grocery bills and so on.

Short-term savings are also often held, giving slightly better interest rates, but not tying up your funds for a long period of time. These can include:

- Savings account – most banks offer some sort of savings account where you can save a certain amount with a higher interest rate for a fixed term.
- An Individual Savings Account (or ISA) – you can save a certain sum every year tax-free. Usually these accounts will allow you to have access to your savings throughout this time, others will be tied in to a minimum term.
- National Savings and Investments (NS&I) plans – these are a series of saving options that are 100 per cent secure as they are backed by the government, they include Premium Bonds and Income Bonds.

Medium- or long-term savings tie up funds for a longer period of time. They can include:

- Trust accounts – a small contribution is made to the account regularly for a long period of time, such as £25 a month for 10 years.

Increasingly banks are offering accounts for children. This began in the mid-1980s when banks offered schemes for teenagers to open accounts, and has scaled down to younger and younger children over the years (NatWest gave away a family of piggy banks in the 1980s and HSBC famously offered a successful incentive of a piggy bank for each child that opened an account with them). Naturally the aim is for children to remain with the bank beyond their childhood years and into adult life. Once a child becomes an adult it is very unlikely that they will change bank accounts; you are more likely to move home than change banks.

Why you need to know these facts

● In the UK, there is a poor attitude towards long-term saving. This is important to challenge as today's children are likely to live much longer than we are. Some statistics suggest that the average age is likely to be closer to 90 than the current 77. Living longer requires additional funding. As a result we should be encouraging children to learn about long-term investments and savings as well as short-term. This will require teachers to understand the benefits of friendly societies, ISAs and trust accounts.

Vocabulary

Friendly society – typically an organised association of people who regularly contribute to funds for financial benefits, health or retirement plans or life assurances.

Individual Savings Account (ISA) – an account that is tax free to a certain limit; considered a medium-term investment account.

Investments – something that money is invested into with a view to future commodity (generally referred to as 'savings' or more creatively as a 'nest egg').

National Savings and Investments (NS&I) plans – these are commonly known as investment bonds but are a series of saving options that are 100 per cent secure as they are backed by the government.

Savings – a commonplace term used to describe an amount of money invested into saving, typically a bank or savings account, with the object of accruing money in a safe place.

Trust accounts – long-term investment accounts usually involving small contributions over a long period of time (for example, £25 every month for 10 years).

Amazing facts

● In 2005, the Guinness World Record for the largest piggy bank went to the PennySaver bank. It was used at the California State Fair for raising money to help support victims of Hurricane Katrina. It is big enough to park your car in!

● Money boxes (or piggy banks) date back hundreds of years. Examples of money boxes have been found in the buried remains of Pompeii and Herculaneum, and a temple-shaped money box with a slot for coins on the altar dating back to the 2nd century BCE, was found in Greece.

● Contrary to popular belief, the piggy bank has nothing to do with pigs. Instead, the name comes from an old English term for a type of clay used for household objects. During the Middle Ages metal was expensive and 'pygg' clay was very affordable. Coins were therefore stored in money jars referred to as pygg jars or pygg banks. Over time the word evolved into 'pig'. They became a very popular children's gift in the 19th century, when potters were asked to make 'piggy banks'.

Sensitive issues

Any discussion revolving around money will, inevitably, lead to a certain amount of 'showboating' from some children. While care and understanding is required the importance of this subject should reinforce the need to teach it rather than shy away from it. If we did that then we would be omitting a genuine life skill.

Common misconceptions

Children are not eligible for savings plans.
In fact there are many different forms from ISAs to Child Trust Funds, friendly society shares to National Savings and Investments

plans. The government offers or supports a range of children's savings plans. Useful advice on the types of plans available can be found by going to www.gov.uk and searching for 'children's savings plans'.

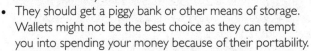

Teaching ideas

● Encourage the children to formulate a savings plan of their own, following these guidelines:
- They must decide what they want to do with the money they save. Ask them to cut out a picture of the item they would like to buy and its price from a catalogue or magazine and stick it on the wall in their room or somewhere they will see it often.
- They should get a piggy bank or other means of storage. Wallets might not be the best choice as they can tempt you into spending your money because of their portability.
- The children should find a place to store their piggy banks, preferably out of sight so they won't be tempted to look and possibly spend their money on other things.
- They should tell someone that they are saving their money so that they can help to keep them from spending it. Make sure it is a trustworthy person.
- The children should remember that *every* penny counts.
- Spending money should be spent wisely. The children should decide on an amount a week to spend, and make it a very small portion of their savings.
- The children could set a budget. They should work out how much they get in a week, and how much they spend. The budget should be placed where they will see it frequently.
- Ask the children to count all the money in their savings. They should make a note of it and come up with a goal which they'd like to meet. Having a goal in mind will make saving easier.
- They could ask other family members if there are any jobs they can do round the house which they can be paid for.

- Set up a class debate. You could discuss the following:
  - What is the advantage of using a saving account?
  - Are you more or less likely to spend your money if you keep it in your purse/wallet or in an account?
  - Should you just be given pocket money or earn it?

Interest

Subject facts

Interest is something that, as adults, we will all be familiar with, whether it's the interest on a credit card, a mortgage or car loan. When considering borrowed money, interest is a percentage of the amount loaned added to it as a fee for using the money periodically (usually monthly). For savings, it is a sum that the bank adds to the funds.

Interest varies according to the risk the lender thinks is attached to the loan – if the lender judges that it involves a high risk then the amount of interest is generally higher. Equally, the type of loan impacts on the interest – long loans tend to have lower interest than short-term ones. Credit cards are, in effect, an ongoing loan that is continuously flexible both in use and repayment. This represents a high risk for banks and therefore the interest is set at a much higher level. Interest is often linked to debt, which is discussed more fully later in this chapter.

The word 'credit' comes from the Latin word *credere*, meaning 'trust' and the word 'interest' derives from the Latin *interesse* which means 'differ, be important'. The amount of interest we pay is generally very important!

Explain that when a person puts his or her money in the bank, the bank is, in a sense, borrowing the person's money. The bank uses the person's money by lending it to other people or companies. The bank *charges* interest to the people it lends money to and *pays* interest to those who put money in the bank.

Why you need to know these facts

● Clear teaching of proper financial management can help children to understand what causes debt and help them to avoid it in the future.

● It is worth sharing the idea of interest with the children. Explain that you will often have to pay back an additional amount, called interest, which is usually a percentage of what you borrowed. For example, if the interest charge is 10 per cent then you pay back £1.10 for every £1 you borrow. This means you will pay back more than you borrowed in the first place. You should make sure that anything you buy on credit will last longer than the repayments. A three-year loan might be a sensible way to buy a car, but it would not be a good way to pay for a holiday. You have to pay back a loan for an item even if it wears out or breaks before you have finished paying the instalments.

Vocabulary

Credit – where a buyer can take something now and pay for it at a later, agreed time.
Interest – payment for the use of loaned money, usually calculated as a percentage of the loan; the measure used to demonstrate the growth of a debt.
Loan – an amount of money given to somebody on the condition that it will be paid back later.
Repayment – paying back money that is owed to somebody.

Amazing facts

● The first credit card was issued in 1951.

● Credit was first used in Assyria, Babylon and Egypt 3000 years ago. The bill of exchange – the forerunner of the banknote –

was established in the 14th century. Debts were settled by one-third cash and two-thirds bill of exchange. Paper money followed in the 17th century.

● The first advertisement for credit was placed in 1730 by Christopher Thornton, who offered furniture that could be paid off weekly.

● From the 18th century until the early part of the 20th century, 'tallymen' sold clothes in return for small weekly payments. They were called tallymen because they kept a record or tally of what people had bought on a wooden stick. One side of the stick was marked with notches to represent the amount of debt and the other side was a record of payments. In the 1920s a 'shopper's plate' – a 'buy now, pay later' system – was introduced in the USA. It could only be used in the shops which issued it.

Sensitive issues

The *Aviva Family Finances Report* for January 2012 found that the average unsecured family debt had risen from £5360 in January 2011 to £7944 a year later. Much of this will have been interest on credit cards. This has a double impact: first, families are generally accruing more debt as a result of interest, and second, families are saving less as a result of higher interest repayments. This is most likely a direct impact of the recession. Family debt is a national issue.

Teaching ideas

● Ask the children what a bank is and why people put some of their money in banks. Elicit from them that two reasons are:
  • to protect the money from thieves
  • to make more money by getting interest from the bank.

● It's important for children to understand what 'interest' means. Define interest as 'a fee paid for borrowing money'. Show the children an example such as:
  • John puts £100 in the bank for a year.
  • During that year, the bank lends John's £100 to Chloe.
  • At the end of the year, Chloe gives the bank the £100 *plus* the interest she must pay, so she gives the bank £108.
  • At the end of the year, John takes out the £100 he put in earlier *plus* the interest it earned, so he gets £105.
Ask the children: How much money did the bank make on John's £100 during the year? Why does the bank charge Chloe £8 but pay John only £5?

● Explain that interest is expressed as a percentage. The bank says to John, *If you give us your money for a year, we will give you 5 per cent interest at the end of the year. So you will earn £5 on your £100.* The bank says to Chloe, *If you want us to give you money for one year, you will have to give us 8 per cent interest at the end of the year. So you will have to pay us back £108.* Make sure the children understand why the bank needs to make money.

● Ask the children to assume that they each earned £100 for a job they did. Tell them to work out which of the following banks to put their money into for one year.
  • Bank of Barton pays 5 per cent at the end of the year to someone who starts a new account. Bank of Barton is within walking distance.
  • Bank of Mill Hill pays 5 per cent at the end of the year to someone who starts a new account. It will cost 50 pence to take the bus each way to make the deposit in Mill Hill and another 50 pence each way at the end of the year to take out the money and interest.
  • Bank of Oxford pays 4 per cent at the end of the year to someone who starts a new account. In addition, it will give you a mouse pad that it says is worth £2. Bank of Oxford is also within walking distance.
Ask the children to explain how to compare the three banks. They should come up with the following reasoning:
  • Bank of Barton – you will have £105 at the end of the year.
  • Bank of Mill Hill – you will have £105 at the end of the year but will have spent £2 in bus fares, so will have

only £103. (Note the bus fare is not to be deducted from the initial amount.)
- Bank of Oxford – you will have £104 and a mouse pad worth £2.

Ask the children to decide which bank they would choose based on the information. The class may split between children who choose Barton and children who choose Oxford (the choice perhaps depending on whether or not a student needs a mouse pad).

● Give the children the following information about three banks in which they could open a savings account (the amount they have to save is up to you):
- Bank of Southgate will pay 4 per cent interest and allows you to check your account by phone or online. The bank is within walking distance.
- Bank of Downton will pay 5 per cent interest on a new account. This bank does not yet have a system that allows you to check your account by phone or online. The bank is within walking distance.
- Bank of Upton will pay you 5 per cent interest. To deposit your money there, you will use the Post Office. To take your money out at the end of the year, you will spend £1 on the return bus fare.

Ask them to work out, in writing, which bank they will put their money in, explaining their reasoning. They need to consider how much money they will wind up making and other factors such as convenience.

● Model using a calculator to work out a fraction or percentage of an amount. Ask the children to use calculators (one per pair) to answer the following questions:
- Can you find 50 per cent of £1.50?
- Can you find ¼ of £2.60?
- Can you find 30 per cent of £3?

Debt

Subject facts

You are in debt when you owe somebody money. Debts get bigger if you are charged interest. Interest is a charge on the original debt. For those caught in debt it can be a highly emotional experience, particularly if there is no obvious way out of it. Debt, however, is manageable and most families will have some sort of manageable debt. The largest is most likely to be a mortgage, but loans used to purchase large items, such as a new kitchen, are equally common (particularly with the rise of 0 per cent interest firms that make the debt appear more attractive, as it is not gathering interest).

Countries and companies also accrue debt. In 2012, Britain's debt was just over £1 trillion. This may seem a lot but compared to America, with around 16 times that amount just in national debt and with $120 trillion of national liabilities, Britain's debts seem quite insignificant. (A 'liability' is both the debt and financial obligation of a company or country.) Probably unsurprisingly global debt has increased dramatically over the last decade. Debt varies significantly from country to country. This is in part down to a country's ability to manage their debt: richer countries can manage more debt than poorer ones. However, when evened out and considered on a personal basis, the average Irish person owes £54,000 compared to the average Vietnamese person who owes just over £700. Britain's debt has risen from £9400 per person in 2001 to over £34,000 in 2012. Globally debt is rising by over £1 million every 30 seconds. It is this extraordinary growth in debt that is challenging global economies to grow out of recession.

Debt, like banks, is as old as human civilisation. The first recorded laws had to do with repayments and repossessions. The idea of debt depends on a common sense of fairness: if you borrow and don't pay back, justice is violated. That is not exclusive to humans – chimpanzees seem to have similar ideas. But debt is not morally neutral. Borrowing too much is a sign of corruption. So is being a merciless lender. Debt metaphors ('overwhelmed', 'drowning', 'crushing' and so on) are dramatic and evoke literary comparisons (Margaret Atwood famously refers to debt through metaphor in many of her books and has written about the subject in *Payback*). Debt gives rise to one of money's greatest metaphors: in the end, money is time, and you may pay with your life – if not through death, then through dull, hard work.

Why you need to know these facts

- It is critical to understand that debt has had an impact on human society ever since it formed itself into a marketing structure, thousands of years ago. The challenge and impact of debt were as important and valid then as they are today. Equally it is important to understand that, for the first time in modern history, our generation and the next will be poorer than the preceding ones. What this suggests is that our children will typically have to borrow more, increasing their debt, in order to maintain the current standard of living. Equally, our parents had to borrow less to maintain our standard of living. The current baby boomers are the last generation who 'had it good'. It is for this reason that educational thinkers are urging governments to add enterprise and financial education to the curriculum in order to provide the current generation of children with the tools necessary to help support them in their lives. An early introduction to what debt is and how to understand it could avert unnecessary personal anxieties in adulthood.

Vocabulary

Debt – an amount (it may be financial or a service or item) that is owed to another person.
Poverty – a state of being poor, and in many cases of being affected by a general shortage.

Amazing facts

- In 2005, the G8 (a group of leaders of eight of the richest countries in the world) agreed to cancel the debts owed by 35 of the world's poorest countries. This helped these countries to pay for thousands of doctors and teachers and to make life better for everyone who lived there. The movement that campaigned for this change was called Make Poverty History. For more information on this unique event and an informed perspective on what happened that year read *Make Poverty History: Political Communication in Action* by Nick Sireau.

- In March 2009 the Bank of England lowered the interest rate to just 0.5 per cent, which was a huge and unprecedented reduction – just three years earlier the interest rate had been just under 6 per cent. However this is nothing compared to Thursday 15 November 1979, when the interest rate was increased to a massive 17 per cent – a 3 per cent rise on just four months earlier.

Sensitive issues

Shakespeare's Shylock in *Merchant of Venice* famously demands a literal 'pound of flesh' in repayment of a debt. It was then, as it is now, a figurative amount. Ironically, people who are caught in severe debt often suffer physically as a result of the stress. So, while they may not have a literal pound of flesh taken from them, the emotional impact of the debt can trigger very real physical illnesses that are the equivalent.

Common misconceptions

Debt is bad.
Often debt is perceived as an evil akin to a sin. The reality is that, in most cases, without debt options we wouldn't be able to afford the house we live in. There are some general 'rules of thumb' about how to manage debt, such as never owing more

than 33 per cent of your total earnings, but the reality is that modern finances have forced this to change. Increasingly people, particularly homeowners, have larger debts and while interest rates remain low this is manageable. However, as soon as rates increase – even by just 1 per cent – it can have a dramatic impact on lives. So, while debt is necessary, the various pieces of 'urban advice' are only good pieces of advice if you can manage the debt you are in for the foreseeable future – a tricky thing to do!

Teaching ideas

● Ask the children to work in small groups to think of some things they think they really need and some things that they could manage without. To help them, they could run through their Saturday morning routine and identify what they did, noting what is essential and what is a luxury. For example: ate my breakfast and watched television; played with my basketball; went for a swimming lesson. The children should talk about their choices and put their ideas in two columns, headed 'Need' and 'Want'. Did any children have ideas that they have difficulty placing? Aim to draw out that sometimes what we think we need is not necessary at all for survival, but makes our life more enjoyable or more interesting. Remind the children that some children live in poverty and do not have either their needs or their wants met. Extend the activity and challenge some luxuries. A mobile phone may be seen as a luxury but can be the single thing somebody needs to lift themselves out of poverty. The phone might provide them with a form of communication that supports their income through work, or may help them to find work in the first place.

● Place these two statements on the board. Ask the children to imagine someone they know has said:
  • 'Sometimes my mum gets really upset when I'm invited to a party because we can't afford a nice present.'
  • 'I don't like it when my friends talk about the latest game consoles – there's no chance we'll get one of those.'
Invite the children to talk about these statements in pairs or small groups and discuss answers to the following questions:

- How do you think each situation makes the child feel?
- How could you help this child feel better?

● As a whole class, the children can now use their group work to draw out how they could apply more understanding at school and at home by being thoughtful and sensitive towards others who are less well off.

Resources

Useful links
www.gov.uk – government services and information.

Reports
Aviva Family Finances Report: January – 2012 (Aviva).

Books
Payback: Debt and the Shadow Side of Wealth by Margaret Atwood (Bloomsbury).
Make Poverty History: Political Communication in Action by Nicolas Sireau (Palgrave Macmillan).
Debt: The First 5,000 Years by David Graeber (Melville House).
Banking Online for Dummies by Paul Murphy (John Wiley & Sons).

Ethics and charity

'Charity begins at home'. In a world of fiscal restraint, schools could be forgiven to sticking to this mantra. Why should schools give money away to other organisations when they are clearly charities themselves? It's a tough argument to ignore but I'd like to suggest that exploring the ethics that underpin finance and then understanding the importance of charitable contributions can perform a number of educational tasks:

● It introduces children to the altruistic world of charitable giving and offers real examples of how to give and the impact of giving (either financially or of our time), providing an opportunity to experience the joy that giving can bring.

● It provides an opportunity for children to understand how finances can be used creatively by another organisation and how, in many cases, a relatively small amount of money can be used to go a long way.

● It provides children with a real window into another aspect of their place within the world, either locally or internationally, that they otherwise might ignore or simply be unaware of.

Defining ethics and charity

Subject facts

It could be argued that not providing opportunities for children to raise money for an organisation or charity is to ignore an important life lesson: giving is as good as receiving! Equally, it risks patronising children's understanding of the world and their possible impact on it. After the Boxing Day Tsunami in 2004 I was approached by a number of our schoolchildren asking if we could 'do something' for those affected by that tragic event. Perhaps they approached me because they knew I would take this seriously and would want to action their concerns. However I think it's far more likely that they simply felt an overwhelming desire to help.

There have been several occasions in my career when I've come across this, either in times of international crisis or where there have been tragic events locally, where children have had an overwhelming urge to help. Each time it has hit me how sensitive children are to events beyond themselves, and how willing they are to invest the huge amounts of energy and enthusiasm they have into doing something about it. And when actioned there is a great sense of pride in having 'done their bit' to help.

Ethics

Ethics is a subject that underpins the very fabric of all schools (either discretely, as stated in your prospectus, or openly within your community – often the true 'lived' ethics of a community). As something that we teach indirectly it is an area that receives less attention than perhaps it should. Yet without ethics not only would the whole financial system crumble, so would society.

While we might like to think that the financial world is full of unscrupulous Gordon Gekkos (Gekko is the wonderfully materialistic bad-guy from the 1987 film *Wall Street*) the reality is that it is built upon social conservatism and as a result it gets very twitchy if it suspects fraud of any kind. For this reason, financial institutions are generally highly ethical and follow the letter of the law (you may not necessarily agree with the law but it is followed). Failing to adhere to ethical practice risks the reputation of any organisation and in the worst cases can see it collapse. This is most clearly demonstrated by a run on a bank, when a whole community has lost confidence in the single place where they felt their money was safest. This was beautifully portrayed in the 1946 film *It's a Wonderful Life*, starring James Stewart as the 'lost' banker. In the film we see Stewart's character, George Bailey, stop a bank run that threatened to tear the company to the ground. Scenes like this sound like fiction but when people fear for their money they can react in uncharacteristic ways (it's happened in Britain and has threatened to happen several times in Greece recently, as it totters its way forward within the EU).

The economist and philosopher Adam Smith is quoted as saying: 'All for ourselves, and nothing for other people, seems, in every age of the world, to have been the vile maxim of the masters of mankind.' People who are obviously greedy naturally repel us and whether a financial institute regulates its own ethics internally or because of the power of its customers, it seems that ethics is a cultural norm that in general humans want to adhere to and, importantly, want the financial market to adhere to.

Charity

Charity is how we, as a community, express our ethical ideals. We give charitably to those organisations that we believe are ethically closest to our community ideals. Unsurprisingly, organisations that are linked to health receive the highest amount of charitable contributions, as personal health is generally the most important area in people's lives, ahead of famine, poverty and the health of other nations. That said, the families of some of the children in your class are likely to have come from other countries. It is therefore wise to appreciate the ethical variances between cultures. Not only will this support your teaching of ethics and charity, it will also impact on your understanding of the class.

Benefits of raising money for a charity

Much of our time is spent raising money for introspective causes that benefit the children of our immediate community. It is very easy to get stuck on this treadmill, just running event after event for the benefit of the school. It led to me overhearing one parent at my son's school saying 'Why don't we just write a cheque for £20 at the start of the year and get this over with?' While this is a slightly cynical opinion it holds some truth. Communities can become a bit numb to constant fundraising. Equally it's not particularly healthy for a school just to look inwards on itself. Raising funds for other causes allows a school to adopt an outward-looking approach. It promotes citizenship within the community and a sense of altruism, and it can be fun!

Your community and beyond

Do your school's aims and vision look beyond the immediate community? Modern communication has, in many ways, shrunk the world. It is a relatively small step to take to go beyond your community's walls. As a result, schools are arguably extending their boundaries of responsibility well beyond the school gates. This is partly unavoidable and the result of a blended, multicultural society that is increasingly mobile and well connected. Schools are becoming more aware of the potential impact they have on their corner of the world, as increasingly diverse social groups are more likely to be personally affected by any given crisis, regardless of its location in the world. Managed Learning Environments (MLEs) are a safe place to introduce children to a wider national and international community. These do not give rise to the safety concerns that other social-style networks do, while at the same time they offer the same type of international community.

Why you need to know these facts

● It's important that children understand what the difference is between ethics and charity (see the vocabulary section for definitions). Simply put, ethics are what we value as basic principles on which to base our community's existence. They are a set of ideals that form the basis of laws and government.

● There will be common values upheld by most schools as, in general, our society agrees on most areas. A typical set of school values may well include:
- respect
- curiosity
- communication
- encouragement
- creativity
- adaptability.

However, what brings these values alive is the aspiration or vision for them. I've helped develop a number of these types of 'vision statements' and, when written, school leaders have sweated over the correct wording to keep the statements as pithy as possible. What I have noticed is how vision statements reflect the times. A few years ago statements such as 'we aspire for our children to know the world and care for it' – in other words, the green criteria – were seen as important. They still are, but what has superseded them has been well-being criteria. I now see statements appearing such as 'children seek to understand themselves and others'. This seems to contrast with the present times, or maybe it simply suggests that people are reaching out and supporting one another when they are experiencing hardship. Who knows? What is interesting is that people are seeking to reach out, and this will be a factor in your classroom and school.

Vocabulary

Bank run (a run on the bank) – when a large number of customers withdraw their deposits from a bank or financial institution because they lose faith in it and believe it to be unstable. This can lead to a bank running out of cash and facing bankruptcy. A run on many banks at the same time results in a bank panic or financial crisis.

Charity – something given to help a person or persons in need.

Ethics – a system of moral principles.

Non-governmental organisation (NGO) – generally a charity (such as Oxfam or UNICEF) working within a country to provide the type of support that a government typically would but is unable to, often due to extreme events such as civil war, drought or famine.

Amazing facts

● In 2000 Joyce Young gave $40 million to the Hamilton Community Foundation, Canada, the single largest donation in Canadian history.

● In 2010 Bill Gates, former Chief Executive Officer (CEO) of Microsoft®, raised the bar by giving $10 billion to the Gates Foundation to develop and distribute vaccines.

- According to National Council for Voluntary Organisations and Charities Aid Foundation, 2011:
  - There are 170,905 charities in the UK.
  - In 2011 the UK gave £11 billion in charitable donations.
  - Most men between the ages of 16 and 24 do not give at all.
  - On average, individuals in the UK give £20 a year.

- In 2011 the USA gave $300 billion (approximately £200 billion) in charitable donations.

Sensitive issues

It was once thought that crisis moments come rarely. Today they seem to occur with alarming frequency. The international crises of recent years, for example the Japanese tsunami (2011), Haiti earthquake (2010), Hurricane Katrina (2005) and the Mumbai floods (2005), have bought people from all over the world together to provide aid. These were tragic events that personally affected millions of people. However, it brought out a quality in individuals that some had thought was gone: a communal sense of humanity. Thankfully these events are still relatively rare, but working in a school that is sensitive to global crises needs careful preparation. When led with care, raising money for a range of external purposes – be it a reaction to a tragic event or a planned charity fundraiser – can reinforce community responsibility in a way that is part of the learning experience of the school. Learning how to respond to our wider community responsibilities is a core learning skill and can draw out abilities and responses in children and adults that perhaps they don't expect themselves.

Common misconceptions

A set of community values must come from the community, not the head's office, if they are to be upheld by the community. Values drawn out of the community – children, professionals,

parents and other adults – are most likely to have an impact at all levels of your institute.

The wonderfully named Harvard teacher, Lynne Sharp Paine, once commented 'It's striking how many companies involved in scandals had a code of conduct. Most people today are sophisticated enough to know that it's easy to put out a code. What's more important is that it is adhered to.' Plenty of organisations have such codes, or aims, or values plastered all across their paperwork, but if these are not adhered to then they are empty promises. The temptation is to throw everything into the code of ethics, but this leads to a struggle to live up to it, which eventually results in its being ignored. As a school you may want to consider your school values. It is likely that they will cover areas such as respect, curiosity, creativity and encouragement (these are fairly universal). It is your duty, as the class teacher, to see that these values are upheld in your classes and it's the duty of the head to reflect these values across the school. It is a useful exercise to regularly revisit your values to judge their impact and validity within school.

Teaching ideas

● Look at your school values – ask the class to identify where they think they can find them across the school. What values are easy to identify and what values need further evidence? Do the children know?

● Consider questions such as: What makes a good pupil? What makes a good teacher? Are the values a part of the school's direction? Is a good pupil a good citizen? What is a citizen? Are ethics different at different times, for example during a war or a crisis?

● What are the most basic ethics that we should all agree on? What happens when people don't agree, and is this wrong or are they simply expressing their freedom of opinion?

Choosing a charity

Subject facts

Raising money for other charities is important as it breaks down the walls of the school and introduces children to the wider community.

How does a school identify a charity to support?

Today's schools consider fundraising to be a significant aspect of what they do during the year. It may be the annual bid to Sport England to top up club resources; it may be a biannual grant application to the Big Lottery Fund or it may simply be the ongoing bids to local trusts for a hundred pounds here and a hundred pounds there. It is a significant enterprise. School associations are also geared up for raising money, with the average school association raising £3000 to £4000 every year, and many raising significantly more than that. Yet even in this age of austerity there is, arguably, a more significant argument for schools to look at raising money for other causes.

There are many national events that will already be on the vast majority of schools' calendars, such as:

- Comic Relief
- Children in Need
- Sport Relief

These are large-scale, regular examples of whole-community involvement, and when a school raises money for them it is something that a community can genuinely feel it is a part of. From a school's point of view there are always plenty of resources that it can draw upon that add value to the fundraising events within the classroom or in whole-school assemblies.

Another standard is the Royal British Legion (RBL) Poppy Appeal. Unlike the previous examples this one is not based on fun and laughter – quite the opposite. It is a sombre reminder of those who lay down their lives for this country. How we handle this message needs careful thought, and there are many resources that have been developed that will constructively support children to reflect on what the poppy signifies. It is an important opportunity to consider something very serious that is part of recent and current history. The RBL have a number of resources on their website and education companies such as Espresso have developed mini topics and assemblies for use in school. The money raised for this charity is small but the message is big.

Community charities

There is a strong likelihood that your school or someone in your school will have a link with a charity or cause. In many cases these will be to do with health-related issues. A recent discussion in one of my classes was on what charity to raise money for at the monthly biscuit sale, it was agreed by the class to give the proceeds to a charity. The children were given the task of researching a charity and then presenting their argument for raising money for it to the class a few days later. It was an interesting task and the class rose to the challenge. Eventually a range of charities were identified, all worthy and all of great interest to the children. It was later decided by the children to split the proceeds between two charities, a local one and an international one. Identifying the international charity took several rounds of voting and there were a few downcast faces, however the decision about the local charity was unanimous – a little-known charity was identified and, because of the support they were giving to a child's family during a family member's illness, they were to benefit from the proceeds. The most interesting aspect of this was how matter-of-fact the children were about it and that it was almost natural to them that money should go to this charity.

Another, very different example comes from a North London primary school. They had a well-established fundraising strategy and as a result a well-established and well-kitted-out school. The decision was taken by the senior management to divert the traditional fundraising effort and raise money for a focus project in East Africa, PlayPumps (a charity that has developed an innovative way of pumping water that encourages children to spin a merry-go-round-style pump in order to draw water). Each pump costs £7000 to build and install, and this is what the school aimed to raise through their traditional school association fundraising routes. They tied a number of additional events to it, where every opportunity to raise money was taken and the money was given graciously. Although the target was to raise the money in 12 months they achieved it much faster. It was an interesting link for the school and one that demonstrated deep financial commitment. Other schools that operate a covenant scheme may consider giving a percentage of that money to an agreed charity in order to actively demonstrate to children the importance of looking outwards and establishing a culture of giving.

Supporting international schools and children

Working with an international school in need allows children to begin to understand challenges in the wider world. Supporting an individual school or child creates a relationship and, once established, a sense of accountability within that relationship. It is not a one-off event. A relationship with another child or school is a long-term investment but one that, when properly managed, can grow.

There are few school or child sponsorship sites. Those that exist often have a Christian bias, such as Worldwide Christian Schools® (www.wwcs.org). The impact these charities have made on millions of children's lives is extraordinary. However if you are considering establishing an international sponsorship relationship it is courtesy to gain your governors' blessing if your school is state funded, regardless of your personal beliefs.

Major UK child sponsorship charities include World Vision, Plan UK, ActionAid and Compassion UK. Between them these charities cover 123 different countries, the vast majority of which are less economically developed. If you are considering child sponsorship these charities are an excellent place to start. (See the Resources section at the end of this chapter for details.)

Having sponsored a child or school it is important to keep any information about that sponsorship current. A dedicated space to display any photographs, letters and pieces of information about your sponsorship will make it tangible and add a human element. This will help children conceptualise what they are raising money for and why.

Why you need to know these facts

● Raising money for other causes and charities promotes an important life skill: empathy. Empathy is the capacity to recognise and to some extent share feelings (such as sadness or happiness) that are being experienced by another. Someone may need to have a certain amount of empathy before they are able to feel compassion. These basic emotions allow children to grow and mature, which in turn gives greater confidence and self-esteem.

● Various governments swing back and forth on the role that communities play within education. Any teacher, parent or child can tell you that it is critical. I've worked in four different schools; each one was the hub of the community. It was for this reason that Children's Centres across the country were linked or sited on school sites – it's a unique service that everybody has to use at some point in their lives. Ignore your community at your peril.

Indeed, it is the community that creates the unique flavour of the school: 95 per cent of what occurs in schools could be replicated across the country, but it is the community within and supporting the school – that final 5 per cent – that makes it what it is. It is this that children when they are adults will look back on with rose-tinted glasses, and not the algebra lesson. Communities are central to a school's character and as such should be treated with respect and supported.

Teaching ideas

● Operation Christmas Child is a seasonal event set up by the Samaritans that is ideal for schools. The idea is simple: children fill a box with gifts, label it and then send it to the Samaritans (there are clear guidelines on what to put in it on the website at www.operationchristmaschild.org.uk). The gifts are then sent to a wide range of international destinations and hand delivered. The boxes are given to the neediest children regardless of nationality, political background or religious beliefs. The programme has supported over 60 million children since 1990 and regularly delivers over a million boxes in a year.

Fundraising

Subject facts

Red Nose Day

Red Nose Day is, for many children, a highlight of the second term. Its cool mix of humour and serious messages has made it a fixture within schools for many years. Not to mention the red noses, of course. It has a clear message that all children and adults understand and with a spread of good causes supported by big names it has always been a success story, even during recession years. Being part of that success creates purpose behind raising money and allows for some wacky ideas to slip into school. There are many ways that you can raise money for Red Nose Day. They include:

- selling red noses in school
- wearing something funny, such as pyjamas, to school or putting on a themed fashion show (eco-fashion or the 1970s)
- a sponsored luxury ditch – who can live without a computer or mobile phone for a week (one for the adults in the community?)
- a sponsored walk to school
- enjoying a sponsored 'bake-off' and then selling the products.

Children in Need

Terry Wogan and Pudsey Bear can only mean one thing – Children in Need. This is the BBC's annual charity drive, its specific focus raising money to support charities especially for children. The chances of a child within your school having benefitted in some way from Children in Need are high. It proves that the adult community in Britain is committed to putting children first.

The Children in Need website hosts a wide range of ideas and resources. Ideas include:

- A sponsored silence.
- Putting on a talent show. Invite friends and family to donate.
- Having a non-uniform day.

- Being sponsored to wear Pudsey ears for the day.
- Having a bake-and-buy sale.
- Having a teddy bears' picnic.
- Dressing in spots for the day.
- Organising a school disco.
- Playing spotty Bingo with your friends and family.
- Guessing how many sweets are in the jar. Ask people to pay to make a guess. The winner gets the jar!

Case study – St Paul's C of E Primary School

St Paul's is a tight community. This may be because it is a small school and well established (180 years on the clock and still counting), and also because geographically the area is well defined. Unusually for North London it is surrounded by green space, which gives a quasi-village feel to the area. When you work at St Paul's you don't just buy into the school ethos, you're buying into the ethos of the community, local church, preschool and pretty much anything else within a square mile. It also happens to be my school.

As head of the school I am gregarious by nature. I like to meet people and I like to know who my neighbours are. After moving to St Paul's, I made it a point to visit the neighbours. I found some lovely people who were receptive to the new kid on the block. What I quickly saw was that this was a split community of the 'haves' and 'have nots'. Within my first week I was taken to an allotment used by the local preschool. It was a fabulous patch of land that had clearly been cared for and was a lovely local space for young children. The allotment itself was divided into smaller allotments that had been themed around various fairy tales: pumpkin allotments for 'Cinderella'; beans for 'The Princess and the Pea', and so on. It was a space that evoked ideas and created memories. The preschool children – many of whom move directly to my school just 50 metres down the road when they reach Reception age – loved it. But this wasn't a jolly; I was being shown the allotment for a reason. It was dying. The preschool had very little spare money to invest back into the allotment and what I was being shown now was a fond memory. I asked how much it would take to bring life back to the allotment. The parent sighed, sucked her teeth and said it would be a lot of money. I was thinking perhaps thousands but it transpired that a lot of money to her was £500. My gut instinct was 'I think we can help'.

Schools have been quick to understand the importance of enterprise. More and more schools are involving themselves in enterprise projects of one sort or another. A local head gives each class £100 and expects that figure to double by the end of the year through enterprise projects – they've never failed; another head runs a radio station with his Year 5 and Year 6 children, who sell advertising space on it with adverts they make themselves. They are all little tricks and fun to do but they have to have a hook. For children, that hook is often altruistic in nature. It is my experience that children are often more generous than adults. Give them a good cause to raise money for and they'll run with it.

I began by floating the idea with my senior leaders. The first question was: How does it fit in with the curriculum? This was quickly followed by: Does it have to? What this revealed, in less than two minutes, was how quickly teaching is changing. We are becoming less tied to national programmes and successful schools are now becoming more confident in experimenting with novel ideas. Yes, we could spend a lot of time tying National Curriculum outcomes to this project or we could go with our gut instinct, which was suggesting that this was a perfectly reasonable way to teach maths, speaking and listening, and social skills. The next step was to identify the year groups who were going to raise the money. Using Years 5 and 6 seemed to provide nice symmetry with the youngest children in the school. We also took the step of mixing the year groups. Each group had between six and ten children and was charged with suggesting ideas to raise money. The ideas were varied and fun. Naturally some were better than others, and some were either too high or too low in ambition. These were some of them:

- Washing teachers' cars – £5 each; target £60.
- A staff meal cooked by the children – £20 a head; target £160.
- Four different stalls at the school fair, each with a target of £50.
- A biscuit bake – £2.00 for every bag; target £80.
- Sponsored homework (a popular choice with some members of the community); target £200.
- A 'Read-athon'; target £150.

While many of these ideas were good, what the children all failed to grasp was the difference between gross and net profit.

They were initially only aware of the gross margin and saw that as the end product. So, while a non-uniform day did eventually net £178 as it had no overheads, the biscuit bake ingredients almost equalled the money raised. Measuring the difference was important if the exercise was to have any lasting effect. The point of the fundraising was to raise money and we were careful not to discourage children from choosing activities that had low yields, though we did discourage any projects that we felt would have negative yields.

We discussed how to run these projects. Some schools run enterprise projects over a half-term while others take a very long view and run them across the year. My personal feeling was that the project risked losing momentum if we tried to spin it out over too long a period. Also, with Years 5 and 6 I was conscious of curriculum demands. It was decided that the children would have only two weeks to raise their money. Points we considered included:

- delegation of roles
- job descriptions
- level of work required (some activities needed more time than others)
- advertising
- financial support and bookkeeping.

Groups were created through a hybrid of friendship groups and carefully selected teams. It was agreed that teams would have to delegate roles within tasks once they were aware of the activity. An activity could only be used by one group – there couldn't be two non-uniform days. Points would be awarded based on how well the groups worked, how successful they were and how much money they raised. The thinking behind this was that some groups didn't have to do too much work to raise a decent amount of money, whereas baking biscuits required a lot of effort, organisation and sales.

To inspire the children and understand how quickly groups can organise themselves we were fortunate enough to be able to access a former contestant from the television series *The Apprentice*. He was able to explain the complexities of working in small groups and the necessity of understanding the impact of different personalities in the group. All of the children were asked to consider what they thought their strengths were and what skills they felt were necessary for a group to work well together. We resisted analysing the responses with the children, but the findings did present some very confident individuals!

The strength of the idea lay in it being a community project. It was something that all the children understood and wanted to support. It has given them a taste of what they can achieve. And we're not alone – local schools everywhere are doing the same thing, and even in these times of cutbacks it seems that schools, more than ever, are reaching out into their communities and supporting them.

Further help and guidance on enterprise in schools can be found in Chapters 5 and 6.

Why you need to know these facts

● Once a school starts down the route of analysing what it raises funds for, it soon becomes clear that in one year a school will be raising money for a wide range of organisations. These may only be pocketfuls of money for each organisation but it raises the profile of that charity within the school community and teaches the children and community the value of reaching out beyond their own walls. What schools could often become better at (although many already do this well) is showcasing the work they do. A simple display of photographs of different fundraising activities, along with letters of thanks, certificates (Children in Need is excellent for this) and running totals keep the profiles of the charities that the children are raising money for high, as well as creating a display that reflects concrete work achieved by the school. The chances are that you already have the certificates and photographs somewhere; it's a great way of celebrating what your school does and keeping people mindful that the school is outward looking as well as focused on its core agenda.

● Raising money for another cause is a concrete example, as any fundraising project has a distinct start and finish with clearly defined success criteria, namely the amount of money raised. It also encourages a certain amount of enterprise and creativity that other aspects of the curriculum are not able to support or reflect.

Amazing facts

The BBC has a long history of raising funds for children's causes, going back to 1927, and on its first Christmas day appeal it raised £1143. This continued with an annual hour-long Christmas day televised charity drive that ran from 1955 to 1979. The present day telethon was introduced in 1980, with Pudsey Bear (named after a town in West Yorkshire) making his first appearance in 1985. It is now firmly a part of the BBC's charitable division and raises tens of millions every year.

Teaching ideas

- Before you decide on a fundraising event it could be worth discussing these questions with the class:
  - Do we currently raise money for a charity and, if so, who?
  - Who should we fundraise for?
  - What are the reasons for choosing one charity above another?
  - Are there some charitable organisations that are more worthy than others?
  - Why do you think Red Nose Day raises more money than other events?

- The Red Nose Day website has a range of assembly ideas that can be used to advertise the day. They explain what Red Nose Day is about, how schools can raise money and what that money goes towards supporting. They are available as PowerPoint® presentations and videos, if your school has a projector in the hall.

- The Red Nose Day website also regularly updates lesson ideas, but a common feature will be a PSHE-linked set of lessons that can be used to explore what Red Nose Day does and how the money is used to support communities. Learning objectives are typically designed so that children can:
  - build knowledge of people living in other countries and understand other people's experiences

- understand their role as active global citizens
- develop ways to express their opinions and views.

These lessons can be found on the website under the 'Schools' tab. You will also find fun ideas to build up to the day, such as:

- sending a postcard to a child in Uganda
- designing a Red Nose Day mobile
- drawing 'word pictures' (for example the word 'cold' drawn in blue with icicles and the word 'smile' drawn to look like a smile to help symbolise the 'before' and 'after' of charitable giving).

Resources

Websites

www.how2fundraise.org – This fundraising website is most useful and offers a range of fundraising ideas and legal advice. Importantly it offers guidance from the Institute of Fundraising in order to ensure that your event is properly and adequately supervised. Where children are included, advice is given regarding providing proper adult supervision, checking that parents and guardians have given permission for their children to take part and carrying out appropriate background checks if adults are to have unsupervised access to children.

www.bbc.co.uk/pudsey – Children in Need – A well-planned event will maximise its impact. To support this, Children in Need have a range of resources that can either be ordered or downloaded from their website, including a planning calendar and fundraising pack.

www.rednoseday.com – Red Nose Day

www.wwcs.org – Worldwide Christian Schools

www.sponsorachild.org.uk – Sponsor a Child

www.operationchristmaschild.org.uk – Operation Christmas Child

www.ncvo-vol.org.uk – National Council for Voluntary Organisations

www.worldvision.org.uk – World Vision

www.plan-uk.org – Plan UK

www.actionaid.org.uk – ActionAid

www.compassionuk.org – Compassion UK

www.britishlegion.org.uk – Royal British Legion (RBL)

Reports

UK Giving 2011 (National Council for Voluntary Organisations and Charities Aid Foundation, 2011) www.ncvo-vol.org.uk

Books

The Berenstain Bears Think of Those in Need by Stan and Jan Berenstain (Random House).

Fundraising for Schools Pocketbook by Brin Best and Ken Dunn (Teachers' Pocketbooks).

Sports Fundraising: Dynamic Methods for Schools, Universities and Youth Sport Organizations by David J. Kelley (Routledge).

250+ Fundraising Ideas for Your Charity, Society, School and PTA by Paige Robinson (Nell James Publishers).

The Easy Step by Step Guide: Fundraising for Your School by Pauline Rowson (Rowmark).

Magazines

Fundraising for Schools (www.fundraisingschools.co.uk)

Films

Wall Street directed by Oliver Stone (20th Century Fox, 1987). Certificate 15.

It's a Wonderful Life directed by Frank Capra (Liberty Films, 1946). Certificate U.

What is enterprise?

Chapter 5

There have been many lessons resulting from the recent financial crisis and subsequent protracted recession. However, it seems that few have made it into the classroom. So, what is enterprise and is there a place for enterprise in education? Are we ready for budding Bransons and savvy Sugars? Arguably there is an appetite for it but first of all we have to understand that entrepreneurial skills are something to value within the altruistic environment of education.

What is enterprise?

Subject facts

Fundamentally, enterprise is about creative solutions to everyday problems. At its most crude, enterprise is another name for business, but at its most inspirational it is about the next generation of Richard Bransons. If you have a good idea the important thing is to get it out to people.

A culture of enterprise is becoming an increasingly important aspect of school life and the curriculum. There is a great deal that children can learn from undertaking an enterprise project but the key rule is to keep it novel. There are plenty of well-intentioned ideas that on the surface sound fun but which are in reality onerous to maintain (the school tuck shop is a classic example). Consider carefully the projects you adopt and understand that some timetabling sacrifices will be needed for the project to work well, but be reassured that it will have benefits that broaden the children's experience within school.

Children are the ones who need to develop the skills required to be enterprising and ultimately they are the ones who will have the energy to drive new ideas forward (with the school's support). Equally, schools are increasingly becoming aware of the positive impact a school council has in the student community: it gives them a forum for their voice to be heard and a strategic influence on the running of the school. Empowering children in schools, when it is managed with care and children are given genuine influence, is an exciting dynamic in school life. It is at its most powerful when a council can confidently manage fundraising events and start to give something back to its community.

However, we tend to limit children's opportunities to exercise their enterprise skills in school. If they are lucky, children today may have the odd opportunity to raise some money for a charitable event but few get the chance to be taught how to structure an enterprise idea or are given the time to do this.

Why you need to know these facts

● For many good reasons, children understand and enjoy enterprise. It is generally a practical activity that demands cooperative learning skills (a good business cannot run itself, a fact that children generally quickly understand) based on a firm real-life situation. Most importantly, children are in a position to quickly evaluate the success and therefore impact of what they have done through the amount raised. The more money raised, the greater the success. It is a simple equation.

Vocabulary

Enterprise – another term for business.
Entrepreneur – a person who has created their own business.

Common misconceptions

Business is driven by business plans.

There is a place for these documents, but only as a guide for the product developer. Business plans are developed by large-scale businesses that are attempting to manoeuvre a very large ship. You can waste a lot of time forcing children to write plans when good discussion can be just as (if not more) productive. The important point is that individuals within a team understand their roles, what they have been asked to do and that they are all working for a common purpose.

Enterprise education defined

Subject facts

The Department for Education and Skills (DfES) proposed the following definition of enterprise education:

> Enterprise education is enterprise capability supported by better financial capability and economic and business understanding. Enterprise capability [includes] innovation, creativity, risk management and risk taking, a can-do attitude and the drive to make ideas happen.
>
> Developing Enterprising Young People (Ofsted, 2005).

This concept embraces future employees, as well as future entrepreneurs. The Howard Davies review elaborated that:

> Enterprise capability [is] the capability to handle uncertainty and respond positively to change, to create and implement new ideas and ways of doing things, to make reasonable risk/ reward assessments and to act upon them in one's personal and working life.
>
> A Review of Enterprise and the Economy in Education (HMSO, 2002).

While the DCSF provided that:

> Financial capability [is]… the ability to manage one's own
> finances and to become questioning and informed consumers
> of financial services.
> Business and economic understanding [is]… the ability to
> understand the business context and make informed choices
> between alternative uses of scarce resources.
> A Guide to Enterprise Education (DCSF, 2010).

Entrepreneurship defined

Within the EU, enterprise is referred to as 'entrepreneurship'.
A broad definition of entrepreneurship education could be
applied, seeing it as:

> …all activities aiming to foster entrepreneurial mindsets,
> attitudes and skills and covering a range of aspects such as idea
> generation, start-up, growth and innovation.
> European Commission's Entrepreneurship directorate

Work-related learning

Work-related learning involves learning *about* work, *through* work
and *for* work:

- Learning *about* work means developing the learner's
  knowledge and understanding of the workplace.
- Learning *through* work is about acquiring practical skills
  in a real working environment, for example on a work
  placement.
- Learning *for* work is where the learner's knowledge and
  skills are developed in a way that is directly relevant to
  the workplace.

Enterprise education is important for several reasons:

- It lets children know that starting and operating a business
  is a career option. This is particularly important for those
  who may not plan to go into higher education.
- It reinforces basic skills in literacy, maths and ICT, and
  relates these to real applications.
- Personal finance capabilities are developed which will help
  children in their work and personal lives.
- It provides a bridge between the world of work and the
  school environment.

- Entrepreneurial individuals are better employees and develop skills that are increasingly in demand among employers.
- It is a motivating approach to learning, developing in the children's self-esteem and a sense of purpose.
- It equips children with life skills and makes them more positive contributors to society.

The most important aspect to consider is that enterprise education is focused on the individual and their potential to achieve. It can be clearly stated that children's aspirations can benefit from this aspect of the curriculum.

Your role as teacher

The teacher is central to the quality of the learning experience.

Children need models more than they need critics to reach new heights.

Anon

Unlike traditional subjects, enterprise education must emphasise attitude and outlook as equal to knowledge and skills. If children are to become enterprising they must change the way they behave when faced with rapid change and challenging circumstances.

An enterprising approach can only be learned through experience and by observing how others are enterprising in their approach. The teacher, as a significant role model, must therefore both design the learning experience and model the behaviours desired. The role of the teacher is as a:

- designer of enterprise learning experience
- manager of the experience
- role model for enterprising behaviours.

An enterprising teacher:

- makes the most of limited resources
- allows the children to make decisions about their learning
- is creative, particularly in finding solutions to problems
- displays teamworking and leadership abilities
- has a clear vision for what needs to be achieved
- is confident and determined
- displays the qualities which they would like to see in the child and can truly say 'do as I do'.

An enterprising teacher is able to:

- create challenging learning experiences for children

- make use of scarce resources to maximise potential
- give children choice and control
- work with a team of professionals from within and outside school.

I hear and I forget; I see and I remember; I do and I understand.

Confucius

The enterprising school:
- develops the enterprising abilities of all children
- delivers a curriculum full of challenge and relevance
- lives the values of enterprise
- fosters application and inspiration
- manages risk
- provides the vision to move forward.

Children are likely to live up to what you believe them to be and what they can do.

Anon

The enterprising student:
- is empowered to make positive changes in their environment
- has numerous opportunities to be creative, make decisions and work with others
- has a sense of purpose
- is determined to succeed
- does not wait to be told
- has a 'can-do' attitude
- is prepared to take risks.

A vision without action is just a dream. Action without vision just passes the time. A vision with action can change the world.

Nelson Mandela

Why you need to know these facts

- Ofsted says there is no universally accepted definition of enterprise learning.

It is often mistakenly regarded as being synonymous with the development of entrepreneurial skills, but an important distinction needs to be made between the two. Entrepreneurship is about starting up businesses, particularly involving risk. Entrepreneurs need to be enterprising to succeed and survive. However, only a relatively small proportion of the working population will become entrepreneurs, while all adults need to be enterprising both in their work and in their personal lives. Businesses need employees who are innovative in their approach to solving problems, can cope with uncertainty and change, communicate well and are able to work effectively in teams. The development of these skills in young people is therefore an essential part of the preparation for adult life.

Learning to be Enterprising (Ofsted, 2004).

• Enterprise education is practical. It is particularly appealing to children who find 'chalk and talk' teaching less engaging and is well suited to Visual-Auditory-Kinaesthetic (VAK) educational environments. Essentially enterprise education is about learning by doing.

• Encourage children to think of as many solutions as possible. Ideas can always be eliminated later in the analysis of alternatives. This makes it difficult to produce model answers: the solutions are only restricted by the student's imaginations.

• Start from the practical rather than the theoretical. Children find it easier to grasp the concepts of analysis and evaluation through hands-on activities. Later they can present their knowledge through written answers.

Vocabulary

Creativity – the ability to use the imagination to develop new and original ideas or things.
Leader – somebody who guides or directs others.
Resilience – the ability to recover quickly from setbacks.
Risk – the statistical chance that something might go wrong or right.
Teamwork – cooperative effort by a group or team.

Common misconceptions

Engaging with enterprise is a bolt-on activity.
It's not. If as a school you are looking at embedding enterprise in your curriculum then you need to show it can thread through the children's learning in the same way as the ICT and literacy 'golden threads'. Many schools try to address educational enterprise by offering one-day or short-term taster sessions. The concern is that these are what they suggest – merely a taster. If as a school you are committed to enterprise then it should be explicit in your curriculum map.

Enterprise in education

Subject facts

So, what do we mean by 'enterprise in education'? Enterprise in education is about taking an enterprising approach to teaching and learning. Enterprise encourages all young people to learn and develop in a way that meets their needs and engenders skills for learning, skills for life and skills for work.

Young people need to be prepared for a world which is changing rapidly. Many of the jobs they will do when they leave school do not yet exist and they will probably have several jobs during their lifetime. They need to have the skills and attitudes to cope with an unpredictable future, to be able to deal with setbacks and disappointments in a positive way, and to continue to learn for the rest of their lives. If we understand this then why aren't we doing it already? And if we are going to do this then what are the core principles underpinning the pedagogy? In essence, the core principle of enterprise education is to ensure young people are well equipped in facing the challenges of the world of work and entrepreneurship, resulting in positive outcomes for individuals, communities and the economy. This involves far more than the occasional money problem in a maths lesson: it means teaching children how to set up a business, market it, delegate roles and responsibilities and find a profit.

Some schools have a very clear understanding and definition of enterprise and implement an enterprising approach to teaching and learning across the curriculum. However, not all schools are at this stage. Many are not clear about what 'enterprise' really means and often they are unaware of the importance of delivering skills for employability and skills required for self-employment. Are we teaching children to 'think on their feet', to value their judgement, to be self-aware, and therefore able to take calculated risks? Enterprise provides a golden opportunity for children to exercise their own interpersonal skills and to think on their feet as they negotiate how their enterprises are managed.

Schools that demonstrate fewer examples of good practice or that are less enterprising tend to connect the word 'enterprise' with entrepreneurship. This can result in a focus on obvious means of making young people more employable. Challenge days, business start-ups, work experience and mock interviews are treated almost as modular, standalone chunks of provision. However, the focus should ideally be on developing broader employability skills through a whole-school approach to enterprise and with provision embedded in each subject in the curriculum. Headteachers need to see the real value of an enterprising approach to teaching and learning, to 'buy into' planning and delivering such skills and knowledge. It is for this reason that Professor Robin Alexander in the Cambridge Primary Review advised that enterprise should be an aspect of the curriculum. So where is it?

Enterprise education is the provision of learning opportunities that help children develop the attitudes, knowledge and skills of the entrepreneur.

Some people see enterprise as a predatory tiger to be shot. Others look on it as a cow they can milk. Not enough people see it as a healthy horse, pulling a sturdy wagon.
Winston Churchill

A whole-school approach

Enterprise education is not a subject, it is a whole-school approach to learning that should be reflected in everything the children experience. Enterprise should be visible in how our learning takes place, the way we work as a school and how we relate to our community.

A whole-school approach to enterprise education will include:

- **Learning for enterprise:** Developing the attitudes and skills of the entrepreneur through a rich and varied curriculum.

- **Learning through enterprise:** Engaging children in authentic and meaningful entrepreneurial experiences.

- **Learning about enterprise:** Raising the aspirations of children and promoting understanding of the role of enterprise in society.
  Every subject has a role to play in developing enterprise ability:
  - the arts to inspire creativity
  - the sciences to foster enquiring minds
  - the humanities to place our understanding in an historical and global context.

Enterprise activities enrich the curriculum and encourage children to take responsibility, make positive contributions and become the enterprising citizens of tomorrow. The children have important roles outside the classroom, and enterprise education means empowering children to make positive contributions to school life: improving the school environment, marketing a drama production, managing events. An enterprising school bridges the gap to the community, forming partnerships for mutual benefit. Enterprise education should begin at primary level and be accessible throughout secondary education. An enterprising school will be at the centre of the business and residential community.

Why you need to know these facts

- The enterprising individual both initiates and thrives on change. Enterprise education enables children to develop confidence, self-reliance and a determination to succeed. These abilities will benefit individuals in their future lives as entrepreneurs, employees and citizens of the global community.

- Enterprise education encourages children to consider self-employment as a career option and equips them with the skills to become a successful business owner.

● Enterprise education supports children in developing the skills demanded by employers in an increasingly competitive economy. Enterprising children have direction, motivation and determination to achieve their goals.

● Enterprise education develops in the student skills in personal finance, decision making and creative thinking. Enterprising individuals have direction and the determination to make the most of challenging circumstances.

Vocabulary

Capital – an accumulation of wealth.
Confidence – a belief in your ability to succeed.
Marketing – a business activity used to present a product or service in such a way as to make it desirable.

Golden rules

Good, enterprising teaching and learning should:
- provide opportunities for learners to think and act in enterprising ways
- provide a clear focus on core and employability skills, and the ability to transfer these to different contexts, in particular the world of work
- provide opportunities for work-related experiences, both within and outside the classroom
- promote positive attitudes
- provide opportunities for learners to develop skills such as problem solving, decision making and risk evaluation
- provide entrepreneurial experiences.

The contribution enterprise in education makes to the personal growth of children is that it can enhance their life chances and choices. It can help them to become successful learners, confident individuals, responsible citizens and effective contributors to society and at work, with a clear understanding of their role in the world.

Teaching ideas

General enterprise-related themes within the curriculum include:

● **Maths:** Financial capability is underpinned by numerical skills. Numerical abilities are also essential in many decision-making situations. Ensure young people are equipped with the knowledge and skills to make informed choices when they face personal and financial decisions at various stages of their lives.

● **History:** The ability to carry out research, evaluate information and weigh up a variety of perspectives is central to making a good decision and is a key skill in enterprise.

● **Art:** Creative thinking is essential for the enterprising individual. Art also develops the ability to visualise, plan and communicate ideas. Working with local freelance 'artists in residence', children can consider financial issues related to being in business as an artist, such as costing created artefacts, calculating overhead and business planning, thus extending the principles of creative projects in your school.

● **Geography:** Understanding of industry and economic development are essential to enterprise. Skills in social enterprise can also be developed, through for example running a fair trade shop where the principles of fair trade are upheld and promoted through the sale of goods. Such a venture can also be supported by work within the curriculum on development and trade.

● **Science:** Scientific breakthroughs are increasingly the source of entrepreneurial activity, for which children will need both scientific spirit and discipline. Creating a school pond, with children being given a budget to purchase plants and materials following research into ponds and pond life, will encourage these qualities. The children can keep simple accounts and bring spending in line with their budgets.

● **RE:** Tolerance and an acceptance of human diversity mean that the enterprising individual works with others, not against them. Social enterprise projects looking at new ideas for charity fundraising and the development of social and economic housing for communities through charitable funding are ways you can explore this.

● **PE:** Enterprising people rarely work alone. PE develops the leadership and teamworking ability needed to ensure objectives are achieved.

● **Design and technology:** Problem solving, working to design briefs, developing a marketable product, critiquing your ideas… this is an enterprising subject in every way. Maybe you could look into designing and producing a healthy eating product for sale, covering market research, budgeting, costing and calculating profit and loss.

● **English:** Writing is an essential tool for an entrepreneur constructing convincing arguments and succinct requests under pressure. Produce a book of short stories or poems written by the children and involve them in business planning, market research, use of accounting software, raising capital, costings and sales.

● **Drama:** Children need the confidence to present to an audience and the presence to hold its attention. Maybe you could get some children involved in managing front-of-house arrangements for a school drama, dance, music or PE event. This could include costing and selling tickets and programmes, and providing and selling refreshments and promotional products at the event.

Enterprise is not a subject in its own right. It is how, within your chosen subject area, you develop innovation, creativity, risk management and risk taking, and above all promote and encourage a 'can-do' attitude and the personal, internal drive to make things happen.

Bridging the gap between schools and enterprise

Subject facts

Much that is taught in schools is hypothetical. There is no substitute for going out and experiencing something for real. That is why so many schools invest time in school trips and guest speakers. The same principle can and should be applied to business.

Organisation for a class trip to a factory is no more complex than for one to any museum or historic building. Indeed, some organisations are well structured and will be able to provide not just lesson ideas but the necessary risk assessments. However, it would be fair to state that in most cases businesses are not as organised as establishments that are dedicated to education. This should not put you off, though. In my experience businesses are only too willing to support visits and in most cases work hard to show off their facility. You may well find that a visit to a local factory or business has been tailored to your needs and provides a valuable platform for your enterprise project.

Equally, inviting a business expert into your school can provide, at the least, an opportunity for children to quiz somebody who is actually doing what they are studying. A useful example of this is inviting a local journalist into class, as their skills are immediately relevant to the curriculum. You may well have other examples that would suit your curriculum. Don't forget parents. There is a good chance that you may have exactly the person you need right in front of you.

Nissan Motor Manufacturing (UK) Ltd

Based in Sunderland, Nissan Motor Manufacturing (UK) Ltd has become a global leader in quality control and efficiency. The plant opened in 1986 and even in its early years Nissan had a commitment to education in the North East. Many of the early programmes focused on engineering skills, as you would expect, but in recent years they have diversified and started to produce resources and programmes that support primary learners. Examples include music festivals, writing competitions and a whole environmental programme focused around the eco-credibility of their new electric car, the LEAF. However, in 2011 the factory staged a unique event, allowing thousands of school children to view it as part of a government initiative called 'See Inside Manufacturing'. This coordinated programme of events across the UK's car industry in 2011 was aimed at boosting the image of UK manufacturing and encouraging more young people to take up science, technology, engineering and mathematics (referred to as STEM subjects in secondary schools).

For obvious health and safety reasons it is not always possible to visit a factory but the example of Nissan demonstrates that opportunities can be made available and that when they are you should take advantage of them. Factories, particularly well organised ones are huge and exciting places to visit. There is simply no way that a film clip on the interactive whiteboard or a 'hot-seat exercise' in class can replicate the scale and detail of a large factory.

Education Business Partnerships

Education Business Partnerships (EBPs) were something that 15 years ago had a lot of traction. Their role is to encourage the public and private sectors to work with schools on a range of projects designed to raise achievement and provide children with opportunities to improve their work-related skills through real-life examples. Schools used EBPs with varying types of projects ranging from engineering-style lessons through to science, maths and literacy. Unfortunately the Literacy and Numeracy Strategies squeezed out much of the time taken by EBPs and their impact on learning waned. However, the opportunities available as a result of a more flexible curriculum are allowing EBPs back into school. It is certainly worth contacting your local EBP; they are often very much a hidden secret.

A number of EBPs have been promoting an enterprise program called MicroSociety. The MicroSociety program is an American learning environment. The concept was created in 1967 as one teacher's effort to restructure his classroom into an academically challenging and interactive place to motivate students to want to learn and succeed. Dr George Richmond, then a newly qualified teacher in New York City, introduced the idea of creating a functioning miniature society in his classroom as a tool to bring relevance to learning and to teach individual responsibility.

He discovered that even the most disadvantaged children realised their potential to succeed when school was made relevant to their daily lives. Ofsted was particularly impressed with this programme and in a June 2011 report (*Economics, Business and Enterprise Education*) commented:

> Five of the primary schools visited in summer 2009 were running the MicroSociety programme that promotes economic and business understanding and enterprise and financial capability, and provides professional development for teachers. The programme involves pupils in Key Stage 2 creating their own society and setting up the institutions required by that society. All of the schools had received high-quality training, resources and support from the Business Partnership which set up the programme. Pupils enjoyed the programme and were fully engaged in the activities. Their self-confidence and self-esteem were promoted well as a result of making their own decisions and running their own enterprises. There was good development of pupils' independent learning, team working, negotiation and problem-solving skills as well as communication, presentational and social skills.

Why you need to know these facts

● You don't need many facts to get an enterprise project off the ground. What you need is energy, a good idea (and with that good research) and commitment. Enterprise is all about tapping what is current and what people want; it thrives on demand. Exciting enterprise projects create demand. They don't have to be complicated and could be simple in scope – if it catches the imagination or is perceived to be needed it will sell.

Vocabulary

Communication – the exchange of information between people, usually spoken or written.
Education Business Partnerships (EBPs) – government-sponsored bodies which link the worlds of business and

education to offer young people a rewarding and realistic introduction to work.

Initiative – the ability to act and make decisions without the help or advice of other people.

Teaching ideas

● Ask children to consider the types of businesses or enterprises they are interested in and try to arrange an appropriate visit or visitor.

Resources

Websites

www.inspiringthefuture.org – Inspiring the Future encourages people from all sectors and professions to work with schools to help young people achieve their potential.

www.myvoicelondon.org.uk – My Voice London is the Education Business Partnership for Kingston and Merton, which provides the training and resources required for teachers to run the MicroSociety project.

www.surveymonkey.com – A valuable online survey tool.

Reports

Developing Enterprising Young People (Ofsted, ref no. HMT 2460, 2005).

A Review of Enterprise and the Economy in Education (The Howard Davies Review) by Howard Davies (HMSO, 2002).

A Guide to Enterprise Education (DCSF, ref no. DCSF–0028-2010, 2010).

Learning to be Enterprising (Ofsted, ref no. HMI 2148, 2004).

Books

Kagan Cooperative Learning by Spencer Kagan (Kagan Publishing).

Inspirational Teachers Inspirational Learners: A Book of Hope for Creativity and the Curriculum in the Twenty First Century by Will Ryan (Crown House Publishing).

Using enterprise

This chapter will consider how children can develop short-term enterprise schemes and will also provide ideas on how children can enhance these skills on longer-term projects, with particular notes on how to jazz up the old-fashioned tuck shop and how to ask teachers to 'move over' and allow children to run the annual book fair.

Getting a business up and running

Subject facts

There are ten common steps needed to get a business up and running:

1. New product development – developing your product and idea.
2. Communication with customers – how the business communicates with customers.
3. Marketing – all types of communication from logos, to adverts.
4. Business opportunities – looking for new opportunities to enhance your business.
5. Teamwork – utilising different skills to make a team stronger and more efficient.
6. Knowing yourself – knowing your strengths and weaknesses and where your skills lie.
7. Leadership – directing a group to achieve a goal.
8. Communication skills – considering all aspects of communication: the message, the sender, the media to be used, the receiver and feedback.

9. Creativity – being able to use creativity to solve a problem or see an opportunity.
10. Taking risks – the ability to be able to judge what the risk is and whether it is an appropriate risk to take.

Why you need to know these facts

● While you are unlikely to set up a full-scale business within school, developing these different skills is important for children to be able to use them in future. If conducting small enterprise schemes, such as a book fair or tuck shop, then these skills will be needed to make a success of them.

Vocabulary

Strapline – a catchy phrase that appears below a main headline.

Teaching ideas

Each step is worth considering as an individual lesson. There are subjects, such as leadership, that we tend to shy away from.

● **New product development:** Ask the class: *What is the latest in communication technology? Where will it go in future, for example in five years' time? What would you want a piece of technology to do for you?* Ask them to sketch a futuristic communication handset and add any specific features.

Then, in groups of three ask them to look at the features they added and to agree which ones should be included in the new design and why.

Now they need to find out if their new handset is wanted by people who might buy it. How would they find out if there is a market for their new handset? Ask them to work in groups to discuss and record three ways in which they could find out. You should expect them to suggest different market research styles, for example an invited panel research, online research via email and showing a demo handset to get reactions.

- **Communication with customers:** Ask pairs to decide on five reasons why businesses and customers communicate with each other. Get the pairs to ask each other what methods of communication would be best for the following situations:
  - You have received a phone message from someone who works in your building. They need an answer to a question today.
  - A potential customer has come to your business to find out more about a product.
  - You have to let a customer know that the item they have ordered has arrived and is ready for collection.

- **Marketing:** Show the children different company logos, some well known and some less so. Explain what a strapline is and give an example. See if the children can think of straplines for the logos. Ask them: *How important is the strapline? What does it do for marketing? What does it fix in the heads of the buyers? Does it influence buyers?*
  Read the following scenario:

> *The tennis racket company 'Strings' has come up with a new thin and lightweight racket. They think it is so unique that they want to market it under a different name and image from the rest of their range. Its features are a strong alloy and carbon fibre frame and a revolutionary new hollow string. They want to market it particularly to young people as a totally new concept in rackets.*

In pairs, ask the children to take turns to tell each other the best points of the new racket and then design a full-page advert for Strings to use in a sports magazine. Make sure they use a new logo and strapline as well as the name of the main company. Remind them to make sure they link the new features of the racket with the new brand, and to remember that their audience is young people and that Strings want their new racket to be a market leader.

Ask pairs to present their ideas to another pair. They need to make sure they explain how their branding fits the new ideas that Strings have and how it will attract the right audience. Ask each pair to give constructive feedback to each other, saying what they think was successful and what might be improved.

- **Business opportunities:** Ask the children to think of a new or updated product they have recently come across – it may be a development of an older product or completely new. Ask them to write down three things about the product that make it attractive to them as a consumer, and then share these with a partner.

   Businesses are always on the lookout for new opportunities. These may involve developing a current product, thinking up and designing a new product, using a new technology, or being able to expand the business in some way. Set out the following scenario for the children:

   Imagine you have a business that makes and sells trainers. One of your design team has come up with the idea of making holiday sandals with a thinner, trainer-style sole with air support included. You plan to call this the Air Sandal. You plan to make the Air Sandal in a range of styles, colours and sizes which will appeal to a range of age groups.

Ask the children to work in pairs to mind map their ideas about how the business can sell the Air Sandal to a wide range of age groups. Digital products are a quick way into this subject. Well-known items such as mobile phones are regularly updated.

   Select pairs to present their ideas to the class as if they are making a sales pitch to buyers for shoe shops. They will have two minutes to make their ideas clear. Hold a class vote on the best pitch.

- **Teamwork:** Ask the children to consider what the benefits of teamwork are. Why do people work in teams? Explain that teams are often made up of people with different skills that, when taken together, help to make the team stronger. What makes a team strong is a common goal and ensuring that, while skills may differ, the goal remains the same.

● **Knowing yourself:** Explain to the children that they are going to carry out a series of activities that will help them get to know more about themselves, their skills and what they need to improve on for the future. Ask them to use the skills list below to help them write down three skills that they consider are their strengths and three skills that they consider they are less strong in. They can work with a partner to discuss and share these.

- generating ideas
- planning and organising
- using initiative
- decision making
- solving problems
- taking calculated risks
- leadership
- teamwork
- setting targets or goals
- communicating and presenting
- adapting to change
- analysing and evaluating
- negotiating and compromising
- managing money and resources
- being resilient
- being an entrepreneur

Ask the children, in groups of five, to share their thoughts about their skills. Their aim is to gather the best five skills for each person so that they know the 'skills total' for the group.

● **Leadership:** To get the children thinking about leadership, first write some quotes from famous leaders on the board. For example:

Learning and Leadership are indispensable to each other.
John F. Kennedy

The art of leadership is saying no, not yes. It is very easy to say yes.
Tony Blair

Innovation distinguishes between a leader and a follower.
Steve Jobs, CEO and founder of Apple Inc.

Ask: *What makes a leader? What are three characteristics of a leader?* Ask the children to share their thoughts with the person next to them and compare their answers. Tell them to be prepared to lead a small group themselves and then work through the following two scenarios.

We Boil for You has developed a new electric kettle that uses half the energy of the company's older designs. In groups, ask one child to act as the leader to get the group to come up with a new name and logo for the kettle, which has to fit with the name of the company. If there is time, the leader will ask the group to start thinking about how they can advertise the kettle.

In groups, appoint one child as the leader. The group has to organise a party in a nursery for eight children aged between four and five. The leader will need to lead the group in a discussion of what they need to do for the party to be a success. By the end of the discussion the leader will have assessed the different skills of the people involved and be able to tell the group what will happen at the party, and what each person in the group will be doing for the party.

● **Communication skills:** Ask pairs to pass on a message using no words (written or spoken) about something to do with a hobby or a favourite piece of music. The partner can ask questions to confirm understanding.

Ask the children how successful they were, and which techniques were most and least effective. Ask them to think of the different situations in which a business may need to communicate a message (for example, internally between leaders and groups of employees and between employees dealing with events and externally between employees and customers).

Ask pairs to discuss the question: *What is meant by communication?* Ask them to think about what is needed to communicate a message well. Write the aspects of communication on the board: the message, the sender, the media to be used, the receiver and feedback. Ask the pairs to think about the most important parts of each aspect. For example, the sender needs to know what they are trying to communicate, the message needs to be clear, the right media must be used (paper, text, email, letter, multimedia message, oral), the receiver needs to be aware of the message and it needs to be clear whether feedback is needed or not and, if so, what sort.

● **Creativity:** Ask: *What are your three favourite foods?* Ask groups of three to share their ideas and explain why these are their favourite foods. Tell them that a food entrepreneur (for example Jamie Oliver) has become very interested in the idea that every area, region or country has some dishes that are produced only there, or that are more popular there than elsewhere. For example: cheddar cheese from Somerset; Yorkshire pudding from Yorkshire; Bakewell tart from Derbyshire; haggis from Scotland. Their challenge is to identify a food that is from their region, culture or religion, or that is popular in their school or family, and then to come up with some snappy marketing ideas, including a brand name, to persuade the food entrepreneur to include it in his or her latest regional cookery TV series. As examples, eggs are often referred to as 'farm fresh' to make them appealing, and milk is referred to as a 'natural' product.

Working in small groups, ask the children to come up with a food theme such as 'Yorkshire yoghurts' or 'Coventry curries' for their region, country, culture or religion. Ask them to prepare a three-minute presentation and a website homepage to communicate their food ideas. Their presentation must say what is distinctive about their foods and why they are already popular. It will then go on to explain how their new ideas will improve the foods and how their website will market the foods well. It would be useful if they had internet access to do this. Select some pairs of children to present and share their ideas with the rest of the class.

● **Taking risks:** Ask: *What is risk?* Discuss the possible risks associated with the following actions and ask them to give a percentage likelihood for each one:
  • crossing the road
  • taking a car journey
  • skateboarding on the pavement
  • buying a lottery ticket
  • getting a job as a lion tamer
  • setting up your own plumbing business.

Discuss what risk means to different people. Provide the children with a copy of the following scenario and read through it together:

The small market town of Normal has a population of about 20,000 people, with about another 30,000 living within 15 miles.

A local entrepreneur has come up with the idea of converting an old brick warehouse into a cinema with two small screens. She also wants to have a fast-food outlet within the building and is trying to get the council to take part in the project by offering them a new electronic library and a car park that they would run and take the income from. She is also trying to get a local group to use part of the building as a nursery.

The warehouse is up for sale for £400,000; the surrounding land for the car park is for sale for £75,000; and the council owns another section of land next to the warehouse.

Her builder tells her it will cost £200,000 to convert all of the building, but only £140,000 for the cinema.

The car park will cost another £75,000 to complete. If the council will carry out the library work and rent the library space, the costs are reduced by £30,000 and the rent income will be £5000 per year.

If she can persuade the nursery to do the same, the costs will be reduced by £30,000 and rental income will be £4000 per year.

Ask: How much will it cost the entrepreneur to set up the cinema only? How much for the other proposals?

Ask them to make a mind map to show both advantages and disadvantages of the project for the entrepreneur.

Planning for enterprise lessons

Subject facts

Subject learning can be made relevant to its real world applications through an activity that draws on problems faced by adults in real-world situations. This approach requires that children work together rather than trying to solve the problem alone. Success is achieved by the way the children work together and the resourcefulness they show as much as their ability.

As in life, the problem may not be clearly defined; objectives must be agreed and information needs to be gathered in order to solve the problem. The children must seek clarity of thought, communicate well and make decisions in order to succeed. This process promotes ownership of the end product. As an example: as a disaster relief agency, how would you manage the resources at your disposal to most effectively support those in need?

Mini-enterprise schemes can be formed within curriculum time, as a cross-curricular, off-timetable project or as an out-of-school activity. Seen as a 'traditional' approach to enterprise education, this aims to replicate the practices of running a small business, including raising capital, selling a product, advertising, marketing and managing the finance (for example, in the course of running a stationery shop in the school).

Enterprise activity can often be undertaken to support an identified need within the community. Children identify the need as part of the curriculum within specific subject areas or within citizenship or PSHE lessons.

This kind of enterprise is often a more challenging experience but equally it can be rewarding insofar as an identified practical need has been identified, researched and then satisfied. As an example: designing and producing a booklet to support basic literacy or numeracy within an infant school.

Historically it has been hard to find anything within the National Curriculum that reflects a consideration of enterprise. It was always a curriculum based on a core set of skills linked to a discrete set of facts, that are therefore limited in their use. This is not to invalidate them – other than a couple of make-overs the curriculum has withstood quarter of a century of changes, though it is now showing its age. Facts can be found in an instant and so the need to learn discrete facts has diminished, in contrast to the need to learn discrete skills and to reflect core community values, which remains largely unchanged. 'Facts' are growing exponentially; simply put, we are capable of 'knowing' far more today than ever before, as a result of the speed of access we have to these 'facts'.

So what are the options? There are a number of writers out there who are considering this subject and how to inject a healthy dose of enterprise education into school life, but with regard to a specific resource the strongest option would be found within the International Primary Curriculum (IPC). The IPC, for those not familiar with it, was a curriculum set up to support international families who found themselves in the position of moving from one country to the next every couple of years or so and who needed continuity from school to school for their child's learning. One of its key values is enterprise – it can be found throughout the curriculum, from Year 1 to Year 9.

There are topics that focus on specific aspects of enterprise such as:

- What people do   Years 1–2
- Young entrepreneurs   Years 3–4
- What price progress?   Years 5–6

However, it doesn't take much digging around to find enterprise links for most themes. Even a topic such as 'chocolate' quickly leads into sessions on the chocolate business, which swiftly moves on to fair trade and what that notion means. A scientifically based topic such as 'mission to Mars' cannot be covered without some discussion on budgets, management and the delegation of roles.

Having enterprise as a core value focuses learning; it creates a filter through which all learning ideas should pass. The common question the teacher should be asking themselves is: Where does enterprise fit into this subject?

Why you need to know these facts

● If we are to value enterprise as something worth learning (and if we have learned anything from the recent years of recession it is that enterprise is valuable) then it needs to be upheld as a core aspect of the curriculum. Only then will educators be looking to draw out the enterprise links and make it an everyday part of a child's learning. While some readers may recoil at that idea, it is in fact something that we do as soon as a child enters school through role play, and we don't have a problem with that.

Teaching ideas

- When introducing the activity:
  - Ensure the children are clear about what the problem is and what needs to be achieved, but do not be too prescriptive.
  - Set a deadline, guidelines and parameters about acceptable approaches, and identify a clear end product that is expected from the children.
  - Introduce the activity as one that requires enterprise skills and thinking, and discuss what you and the children understand by this.
  - Involve the children in developing and setting the success criteria upon which they are to be assessed.
  - Discuss possible introductory steps, such as the allocation of roles, defining the problem and considering an action plan.

- To ensure progress:
  - Avoid directing the process; instead act as a 'critical friend', asking for clarification and justification of proposed solutions. Suggest a way forward if there is difficulty in finding a solution.
  - Ensure that the group has identified someone to monitor progress towards a satisfactory end product.

- To sum up and review:
  - Encourage dialogue about how the group acted and how the process developed towards the production of the end product.
  - Put in place and encourage self- and peer-assessment of the enterprise process as well as individual and team performance.
  - Bring the lessons identified by the groups together and use them to strengthen the children's understanding of the importance of teamwork and the enterprise process to producing a satisfactory end product.

How to organise enterprise

Subject facts

There are many different ways to set up an enterprise and different tasks that the children could do. Some of the main principles needed to start an enterprise are:

● **Demand:** Make sure there is demand for the idea. How much initial enthusiasm is there among staff, governors, parents and children? If it's not there then it won't work.

● **Market research:** Children will need support when undertaking market research but it is vital to do it in order to gauge:
  • the level of demand
  • whether the end-user would buy/use a product/service
  • their spending power
  • the level of commitment from staff, children and parents.
Traditional methods, such as a survey clipboard, are always good. However, if you are familiar with online survey systems (www.surveymonkey.com is a common and easy-to-use facility) you can survey parents on this subject to make them feel included (as it is likely to be their money the children are spending).

● **Responsibility:** Is there a member of staff, governor or parent willing to take responsibility for the initial planning? It will usually be necessary for at least one key adult to take charge in the initial stages. Who do you employ? If there is a great deal of interest then advertise the jobs and invite children to apply for the positions. It is important that they fill in an application form and that, if successful, they attend an interview suitably dressed. The interview should be no longer than three minutes (some children will be visibly shaking throughout the process) but should involve a panel interview with around four questions. Ask the children:
  • What qualities do you feel you have for the job?
  • What would you do if somebody accused you of giving the wrong change?

- What would you do if you saw somebody stealing from [the enterprise]?
- Why do you think it is important to have [the product/service] in school/available?

This may seem very formal but the experience is very important and offers the young entrepreneurs real-life experience in a controlled and safe environment. Once the enterprise is established adult involvement can be minimal.

- **Other considerations:** Are there any school policies that might influence what is sold or how? Are there any issues to be addressed if children are bringing money to school in order to make their purchases? Traditionally schools run a cash service; others take orders and money at registration; some even use a token system whereby parents buy and distribute tokens to the children so they are not carrying money in school (this is an excellent example of a 'promissory note' – it works in a very local environment but in the same way as any legal tender).

- **Location and sales:** Consider where and when the product/service is sold. The key lesson here is to sell what the customer wants, not what it is convenient for the shop to sell.

- **Marketing:** It is critical to promote the enterprise. Newsletters, posters and assemblies are all good ways to market services – but you need to consider the most appropriate marketing for the product/service you are selling. Businesses spend billions on advertising in order to sell their products and until the enterprise is established it is important to keep its profile high. Borrow ideas and search the web, and tell other schools about your ideas.

- **Pricing:** Ensure you have a price list and decide who will handle the money if you decide to use cash. A note of caution: cash is easiest to use but easiest to lose. It is very easy for children to cry 'someone's stolen my money' when in reality they have simply lost it. Consider this carefully or use one of the ideas suggested previously as an alternative to cash.

- **Sell to make a profit:** It is important to monitor how sales are going. Ensure that the children always maintain a daily sales record from which you can analyse sales patterns. An enterprise is meant to model a business and as such must make money. This is a critical element of the enterprise and to lose sight of this risks a failure to communicate the point of running a business.

- **Rota:** It will be good to rotate jobs, giving everyone a chance to carry out each of the different roles involved in running your enterprise. Also make plans for younger children to be involved and learn what to do, then when older children move up the enterprise can continue to run smoothly.

A dedicated person is required to be responsible at the beginning for purchasing, operating and selling, as the project develops the children will take ownership and increasingly run the enterprise themselves. However, the initial champion will have a lot of work to do in the short term.

Why you need to know these facts

- Enterprises can be hard work, but the benefits can often be seen, for example, when running a tuck shop:
  - behaviour in the playground improves when the tuck shop is operating
  - children are better behaved and queue for food in an orderly manner
  - children have increased their responsibility in terms of handling money and have improved their mental calculation skills
  - many of the younger children have had no experience of dealing with money, and the tuck shop provides a safe environment for them to gain experience of shopping.

- Children will always enjoy spending the proceeds. Targets are always good incentives and if the enterprise team make enough money to purchase the targeted resource then it is important to celebrate this in the school newsletter. Alternatively, invite a local reporter round and celebrate the initiative of the children in a good news article in your local paper.

- 'Tuck shop' is a general term for a grocery store in Australia and New Zealand.

- The term 'tuck shop' is believed to originate from around 1780, when the Tuck family opened a chain of general refreshment stores across England.

Handy tip

Watching an episode of the BBC's *Young Apprentice* can provide clear examples of how to work as a team when under pressure. It is important that children understand that within a professional environment they may well be working with people they wouldn't necessarily socialise with. The *Apprentice* programme model shows, generally, how this can work and that, when a group are working on a shared project, provided everyone understands their roles, they can all work together for the common good. Obviously the programme is famous for showing the reverse, but *Young Apprentice* is more carefully edited than the fully fledged adult version – though the situations and problems encountered often seem to be the same!

Teaching ideas

- Work with the children to set up a school tuck shop.
  - Firstly, establish whether there is a demand for one. It is better to start with a tuck shop operating once or twice a week rather than five times a week if you want to maintain enthusiasm. You also need to ascertain the number of potential customers for the tuck shop. Again, if it operates every day then the chances are that, due to familiarity, the popularity of it will wane. You may want to establish a pop-up culture where the shop runs for

two days a week for just one half-term. That way you will guarantee sustained energy around the tuck shop and it will look busy.

- A tuck shop does not need many children to run it. Certainly, it is not a project for 30 Year 6 children, typically you would need three salespeople each session. Many successful tuck shops operating in primary schools are run almost entirely by the children.

- Do some research: What do children currently eat at break times? Is any food currently sold in school other than for school lunches? To run a successful tuck shop, you may need to address issues such as children carrying cash or bringing in their own, say, chocolate and crisps to school. It is for this reason that a tuck shop that operates for limited periods is more appealing as it is easier to maintain existing food policies. The tuck shop is the occasional treat, not the standard. If this is likely to be a problem you could consider running a fruit tuck shop before school or collecting money weekly or half-termly, for example.

- What to sell? Not that long ago there would have been a lot of pressure to sell only healthy fruit snacks. Today, there is a rich variety of snacks that are both healthy and fun. If you are near a cash and carry then it is worth taking the tuck shop team with you to look at the products available and match them against what market research suggested. (If you are going to do this then contact the shop before bringing the children, as sometimes these stores don't allow children.)

- Most schools run the tuck shop at break time but some run it before or after school. If you have a range of school clubs you may decide to run a tuck shop during that time, however there is a fine balance between an enterprise project that produces a small income and what could be interpreted as taking any opportunity to extract money from families.

- Decide how to run the tuck shop. Some schools use the school hall, a classroom or a table in the playground. The site needs to be accessible so a sheltered spot in or near the playground is ideal. You may want to limit the customers to particular days. For example, Monday could be Years 5 and 6 and Friday Years 3 and 4. This will allow the shopkeepers to adapt their product range throughout the week, as children in different age groups may prefer different items.

- Plan where you will store the stock, some of which will be perishable. Usually a cool, dry storeroom will be adequate. You will need to discuss this with your site manager. Use this to introduce the importance of food hygiene and the potential health implications of poorly stored food.
- If you are selling fresh items then plan who will wash fruit and vegetables. Sometimes fruit or vegetables will need cutting or preparing in some way before you sell them. Ensure that those handling the food always wash their hands. An adult must supervise this work, following health and safety guidelines on preparing food and the use of food preparation equipment.
- The promotion of the tuck shop should be a partnership between children and staff – if the head teacher endorses it in their newsletter this will give confidence to the children involved in marketing. Make seasonal changes to the produce, to keep interest up.

● Have competitions for children to design and make advertising posters. Send letters home to parents to let them know about the tuck shop. Try a range of incentives such as:
- two for the price of one
- loyalty cards
- a free sticker with every portion of fruit.

● You could link your tuck shop work to other areas of the curriculum:
- Science projects about nutrition and plant growth.
- Geography lessons based on the country of origin of fruits and so on.
- Sales figures are a good real-life data source to link to the maths and IT curriculum.
- Once the tuck shop has been established for an extended period of time the children could predict the use and therefore potential income from the service for the entire year. Trends could then be followed and stock increased, decreased or changed altogether to match demand. Where there are unanticipated dips in business, predictions

can help gauge what potential profit has been lost. Equally, if the profit is being used for a particular item then a robust and checked prediction is necessary to ascertain if the profit for that period is on track. The children would also be required to carry out market research, contact suppliers, coordinate and promote the service; and monitor sales. This is also a real-life opportunity for using mathematical software programs such as Excel, in which children can create formulas in order to make predictions and to assess whether sales have increased or decreased against those predictions.

Creating 'enterprise' teams

Subject facts

Teams are often made up of older children, typically Years 5 or 6. However, this needn't necessarily be the case. In most situations basic mathematical skills are the only requirement and, with support, children in most year groups should be able to run a fundraising activity.

As with any aspect of learning, children will need to be taught what to do. The level of teaching requirement will depend on the activity that you have in mind. You will need to unpick the various stages involved in the activity.

Consider what skills the children will need in order to be effective team players. A reasonable size for any team is four to six, as this will allow for responsibilities to be shared. Teams larger than this can result in some children not having an active role. Equally, teams with fewer children can put too much pressure on children. General roles could include:

- a leader who coordinates the team and ensures that all team members understand their task
- a liaison officer who liaises with any significant adults
- a bursar responsible for finances
- a marketing officer who leads the marketing effort
- a researcher who leads enquiries into the various activities children would want to be involved in and how they would like them delivered.

There is no more meaningful assessment of success than an amount raised. This is the benchmark that businesses use for monitoring purposes and it is one that children easily understand. If you are involved with the organisation of teams it is worth setting a reasonable financial target with the children; it is that target that enables them to judge whether they have been successful or not. In either case, children should be encouraged to think about what went well and what could have been done better.

Running a book fair

For decades children have loved being able to choose their own books and to share that experience with their friends. A book fair is a great opportunity to promote reading – of all materials – as a shared experience that almost everybody at some stage enjoys. Book fairs (those run by Scholastic are the ones we will focus on for this case study) and book clubs (also run by Scholastic) are a win–win for schools. They raise money while selling something much more meaningful: the enjoyment of reading. Involving children in your fair will not only increase its chances of success but promote valuable life skills – for years they have been run by staff when it is well within the capabilities of children to run such events.

The purpose of each and every Scholastic Book Fair is to give a child the chance to see, touch and fall in love with the very best children's books. They provide an exciting opportunity for schools to create a fun and inspiring focus on literacy.

For children, running a fair has far greater value than simply reading the books. A Scholastic Book Fair can introduce children to real-world skills within a real setting: they will be counting money and seeing how well their efforts have paid off financially. Running a fair, therefore, offers opportunities to learn about:

- financial awareness
- time management
- creative thinking
- responsibility
- teamwork.

The fair will allow children to develop and practice business skills and learn about the world of work in a safe environment, with the additional benefit of strong links to the National Curriculum in the areas of financial education, mathematics, ICT, and PSHE and citizenship.

Giving the children a personal investment in the project's success, can create a real buzz, involving more parents, children and school staff and giving a boost to your Book Fair – which ultimately means more free books and teacher's resources earned for your school.

Recruiting volunteers

There are many ways to recruit volunteer children. The adult leading the project will need to create a buzz. This can be done by:

- putting up the Scholastic Business School teaser poster (bookfairs.scholastic.co.uk/business_school)
- announcing the project in assembly
- placing a notice on the school website and in the newsletter
- sending a letter to parents outlining your plans for recruiting children to run this year's fair.

You will need to consider what jobs you are going to advertise. You may want to consider roles for a number of teams, such as:

- a team responsible for marketing, that may have little to do with the fair when it is on but will have a lot of work to do beforehand to promote it
- a sales team responsible for the book sales during the fair
- a Scholastic liaison team who will communicate with Scholastic to organise delivery, what titles will be delivered and how the commission will be arranged after sales.

Job descriptions that you may want to use (that are discussed in more detail later in the case study) could include:

- Book fair managers to help coordinate work schedules and ensure tasks are being completed on time.
- Advertising specialists to spread the word about the Book Fair using a variety of media, including posters, letters and emails.
- Customer service assistants to help customers with their enquiries and purchases in a pleasant, polite manner.
- Accountants to oversee the money-handling process and calculate Book Fair takings daily.
- Display specialists to create a pleasant, friendly and fun environment for Book Fair customers to browse in.
- Events coordinators to create excitement at the Book Fair by running a competition and other fun events.
- Browsing supervisors to organise browsing sessions for all classes.
- Inventory specialists to monitor the stock of bestsellers and ensure that customers can order copies if they choose.

Once children have reviewed the jobs available, they'll need to apply for the ones that most appeal to them.

Applying for volunteer roles

You will know the children and understand what they will respond to best. The point of this exercise is that they are attempting to promote themselves as a strong candidate for their chosen job. Set a closing date for applications (don't make it longer than a week) and ask the children to do one of the following in class or as homework:
- write a formal letter of application
- fill in an application form (this is best done as homework).

Interviews

Set up a short, five-minute interview with each applicant.
- Provide job profiles so the children can prepare.
- Ask questions such as: Why did you apply for this job? What skills do you have that would make you ideal for this job? What would you do if… (choose a likely Book Fair scenario)? How well do you work in a team?
- Assign jobs to the children, choosing at least two per role so that they can support each other.

Inform the children of the outcome the same day. If you can, put it in writing: this will take more time but a short congratulatory letter is important and will be something that they will take pride in showing people.

Planning your Book Fair

About six weeks before your Book Fair, you'll receive a call from your Book Fair coordinator to discuss plans. If you have a liaison team of children they can discuss the plans with Scholastic, who will be able to offer advice and support before, during and after your Book Fair.

Bring your team together to discuss ideas about goals, advertising and ways to create excitement, and – most importantly – to clarify who is doing what and when! The following are just a few suggestions and ideas – arranged by job – that your team can discuss and start to plan.

● **Book Fair managers:** Discuss specific Book Fair goals and how best to achieve them, whether they're boosting attendance, increasing book sales or creating a literacy focus. Create a rota so that everyone knows when they need to be at the Book Fair. Plan how to record the project using photos, journals or videos.

- **Advertising specialists:** Aim to build excitement and awareness using letters, flyers, posters, emails and the web. The 'big red box' containing advertising will arrive soon but you might be inspired to create your own. Consider making name badges and t-shirts for the Scholastic Book Fair team.

- **Customer service assistants/accountants:** Create a list of what will be needed at the cash desk. Estimate what change will be needed for the cash float. Children will require training if they are going to accept card transactions (and for the peace of mind of parents it would be advisable that an adult is supervising this, as card transactions are potentially greater in value than cash).

- **Display specialists:** Plan how to decorate the Book Fair using balloons, bunting or special displays. Use a current theme to make the Book Fair fresh, fun and appealing. Draw a diagram to show the Book Fair's location and how it will be safely laid out.

- **Events coordinators:** Choose a competition to involve the whole school. Visit bookfairs.scholastic.co.uk/win for the latest competitions or come up with your own. Hold special events during the Book Fair, such as a fancy dress day, a raffle or storytelling activities.

- **Browsing supervisors:** Create a timetable for class browsing visits. Decide who will collect the children from class and who will supervise them.

- **Inventory specialists:** Review the book selection and plan special table displays for 'highlight' titles.

Your team should now be primed and ready to go. Make sure that everyone knows what they are doing and when.
- Start a daily countdown in assembly.
- Put up posters around the school.
- Send invitations and letters home to parents, stating your Book Fair goals (Scholastic will provide template versions but a letter written by the children is always more compelling and personal).

- Put a notice on the school website and in the newsletter.
- Launch your chosen competition to the whole school.
- Download the free £25 book voucher to use for competition prizes.

Running your Book Fair

Below are a list of tasks, tips and ideas for each team designed to ensure they understand what they are expected to do and so that the fair runs smoothly:

● **Book Fair managers:** Ensure all volunteers know what needs to be done and help out if necessary. Put up the goal chart and update it daily (this can show number of books sold, total sales or number of customers). Start to record the set-up and operation of the Book Fair for the evaluation project.

● **Advertising specialists:** Announce the Book Fair's arrival in assembly. Put up the directional arrows and outdoor banner (which are generally supplied by Scholastic in the big red box).

● **Customer service assistants:** Lay out the cash desk with cash float, calculators, pens and a credit card machine (if supplied). Prepare the price list so that customers can place orders and check prices. Record all sales and orders clearly so that daily takings can be worked out by the accountants.

● **Accountants:** Ensure that the cash float is safely collected from and returned to the school office each day. Calculate daily takings, working out sales in cash, cheques, credit and debit cards, and vouchers. Share the daily takings with Book Fair Managers so that progress towards the goal can be updated.

● **Display specialists:** Put up the header boards and use the bookstands to highlight bestselling titles. Decorate the Book Fair and arrange the poster, stationery and hand pointer boxes.

● **Events coordinators:** Collect the competition entries, choose a winner and award the prize vouchers. Create a display of the competition entries at the Book Fair for parents to see. Host an official Book Fair opening ceremony, with the honours going to the head teacher, a local MP or a costumed character.

● **Browsing supervisors:** Collect and return each class on time for their browsing sessions. Help children with their choices and ensure that the books are tidy at the end of each session.

● **Inventory specialists:** Put last copy bookmarks in the bestselling titles to help with customer ordering. Compile a daily bestsellers list by using the sales record sheets.

After the Book Fair

Once your Book Fair is over, there will still be plenty of jobs and tidying up to do. The following are some job pointers for your volunteers.

● **Book Fair managers:** Update the goal chart and communicate the final achievement to the school and parents. Hand out evaluation forms to the team to find out their thoughts and ideas for improvement.

● **Advertising specialists:** Take down any posters, arrows or banners. Put a notice on the school website and in the newsletter letting everyone know the results of the Book Fair.

● **Customer service assistants:** Ensure all customer orders have been passed to the Inventory Specialists.

● **Accountants:** Calculate the final Book Fair takings and communicate them to the teams. Complete the online Cash Report Form to see how many Scholastic Rewards have been earned (bookfairs.scholastic.co.uk/free_resources/cashreportform).

● **Display specialists:** Take down the header boards and place any displayed titles back on the bookcases. Remove decorations and pack away the poster, stationery and hand pointer boxes.

● **Events coordinators:** Send your competition entries to Scholastic for another chance to win.

● **Inventory specialists:** Ensure that all customer orders have been placed with Scholastic before the Book Fair is collected (call 0800 212 281). Deliver customer orders when they arrive.

Finally, once your Book Fair has made enough sales to earn Scholastic Rewards, you can start choosing books from the cases.

Allowing your volunteers to select books for the library or their class is great way to thank them for their hard work. Just keep a note of what has been taken so you can add the total to your online Cash Report Form.

Track your commission rate. If you have been running fairs you should have a fairly steady rate. If it changes significantly you should consider what caused those changes so that they can be replicated (if positive) or avoided (when negative).

Timing is extremely important. Parent consultation weeks are good times to run fairs (as a reward for a good consultation or incentive to do better); October and November are in the natural run-up to Christmas, when parents and carers are looking for presents; World Book Day in March is often a heavily over-requested time for Book Fairs, however Book Week in May is a good time to promote summer reads.

Why you need to know these facts

● Involving children in fundraising activities is an important opportunity for them to learn good life skills. Children understand the importance of fundraising and, when asked, will readily give up their time to be involved.

● Having a clear purpose for the Book Fair is more likely to make it a success, and using a child-led team creates that purpose. People generally want to give money when there is a genuine reason to do so, but equally they want to get something back in exchange. A Book Fair can meet both needs. By advertising its purpose (to restock the library, enhance class reading corners or pay for packs of group readers, for example) you raise its profile, thereby increasing the chances of it being successful.

Sensitive issues

As you may well expect, not all children will interview well. You need to make a decision on how you are going to manage a potential failed candidate. In my experience if too many children have applied for the jobs it is better to create more teams, with different teams allocated to different days, than to turn a child down. This is, after all, a role-play scenario and a 'second chance' goes a long way. Think very carefully about failing a candidate, as they will, despite any apparent 'cool', have put a lot of effort into the application. After all, they did apply, and this is never done lightly.

Handy tip

● You'll need to offer guidance but the children will be ready to step up and take ownership of the Book Fair. Don't hesitate to give them important responsibilities. You can check on everyone's progress at weekly catch-ups.

● Give your team some time to browse the Book Fair before it opens so that they can familiarise themselves with the titles and help customers more efficiently.

Teaching ideas

● The types of activities that children can manage in teams are:
  • Summer fair stalls: Small teams of three per stall. These are great opportunities to see future stallholders in action.
  • Auctions: Two teams could manage the actual event with adult support. Children are naturally persuasive and can elicit that extra pound from the crowd quite quickly. Being the auctioneer will also give them a direct sense of having raised a great deal of money themselves.
  • Breakfast events: A team can run a 'healthy breakfast' where children pay £1 for a light, healthy meal before school starts. This can be linked to other activities such as cycling to school – a further illustration of the links that enterprise schemes have with the curriculum.

● Plan and run a Book Fair following the guidance in the Subject facts section above.

The future of enterprise

Subject facts

'Why teach about enterprise skills in primary school at all?' is the most common question asked. Time is limited and when the lion's share of the curriculum is taken up by maths and English there isn't a lot of space left for other subjects (particularly if you are attempting to design a 'creative curriculum').

The whole subject of enterprise was considered in a recent Ofsted report (*Economics, Business and Enterprise Education*, June 2011). Ofsted concluded that the Department for Education should:

> ...as part of its National Curriculum review, consider the place of well-planned provision for enterprise education (that is, the promotion of economic and business understanding and enterprise and financial capability) at all key stages; so that young people leave school well-informed and well-prepared to function as consumers, employees, potential employers, and to contribute as citizens to the complex and dynamic economic, business and financial environment in which they live.

And later the same document, which praised the achievements in secondary schools, noted in relation to the primary sector:

> Despite the strengths observed, over a third of the primary schools visited did not have a coherent approach to the provision for economics and business understanding and enterprise and financial capability across the curriculum. As a result, they did not ensure that these aspects of learning were well integrated and fully embedded within the curriculum or that they were designed to ensure a progressive development of understanding and capabilities. This was compounded by the fact that, in four of the 28 schools visited, no particular individual had responsibility for overseeing pupils' development in this area. Learning outcomes were generally not being made explicit and were not being assessed in half of the 28 primary schools visited.

While tuck shops and Book Fairs represent clear, obvious business models, the way young entrepreneurs are making money today is different as a result of the web. The music industry in particular has changed over recent years, and it is now far easier to produce a high quality piece of music, take it to market and distribute it globally than ever before, thanks to global music sites such as iTunes®. Schools needn't just create the odd Christmas CD (with the unsold copies languishing in the back of the headteacher's cupboard) with the opening up of the ICT curriculum music can be written and recorded, marketing material (such as covers) designed and distribution organised with relative ease. As with anything like this there will be a cost but if you use a distribution centre such as TuneCore you can reduce your costs. There is no reason why children shouldn't be managing this project and they will want to see effective distribution for the highest impact (expect to be asked to attach any web link to a school text or email for quick download by the parents). It is highly likely that a school will make more money from this form of music distribution than they were ever able to from sales of CDs, as extended families and friends (particularly those overseas) can instantly access the music for a small fee.

There are also various ways to self-publish a book, from a physical paperback to an ebook. There are more and more examples of very successful books that have been self-published as ebooks, and this fact alone is forcing old-school publishing houses to re-evaluate how they publish. Amazon® has been leading the field in this area and offers ways of self-publishing either directly to their Kindle® ebook devices (Kindle® Direct Publishing), which creates a digital version of the book, or through their CreateSpace® self-publishing centre, which will create a printed version of the book. Both offer support on how to market the book, what design to use and how to price it. The Kindle programme, in particular, gives the same instant satisfaction as distributing music through TuneCore. Publishing ebooks is generally free, with the writer (in this case generally the school, but it could be individual writers) claiming 70 per cent of the royalty. A class of 30 selling an ebook of children's poetry at £5 per copy (the price of a typical paperback) could expect to receive a royalty statement for around £105 if each child's parent or carer bought the book. This figure could increase if relatives and family friends also bought the book to support the child or school.

Why you need to know these facts

● The use of the internet is changing the way enterprise and entrepreneurs make money. By looking at ways to use technology to work on small enterprise ideas will help the children learn about these areas, as well as learning new skills.

● It is arguable that we are creating a new subject area, but it is a critical one for our future if, as a country, we are to prepare our children for a new era of enterprise. Other countries across the world have been preparing for this, with China and India taking the lead. Certainly there are still many people within these countries who are extremely poor, but many are taking the new opportunities provided by entrepreneurial thinking. Surely our children deserve the same sense of optimism? As teachers, surely we need to consider how we can share these skills and weave enterprise into our curriculum? Chapter 6 considers this very question.

Amazing facts

There have been many actors who have become millionaires before leaving primary school (such as Macaulay Culkin in the 1990s – he wasn't the first and won't be the last), but Jonathan Manzi is the youngest to make his first million in the business world, doing so by the age of 16 through a web-based business. The internet has created an opportunity to eliminate age discrimination against younger businesspeople. The clearest example of this is Mark Zuckerberg, the founder of Facebook®, who became a billionaire by the age of 23.

Teaching ideas

● Use an enterprise team to put together a school CD. They'll need to plan what it will contain, design the packaging, work out the costings and arrange marketing and sales.

- Create a physical book (see Scholastic's We Are Writers programme) or an ebook. It could contain class work or be a specific project (such as a recipe book). Copies can be sold to family and friends.

Resources

Websites

www.surveymonkey.com – A valuable online survey tool.

www.enterprisevillage.org.uk – This website has been developed to enable teachers to access a free online resource to assist them in developing school businesses and to share ideas and expertise with each other. Originally set up for secondary schools, it now supports the primary sector.

www.premierleague.com – The Premier League Enterprise Academy is developing a sustainable model, enabling Premier League clubs to foster enterprise among young people, principally in deprived areas.

www.surveymonkey.com – A valuable online survey tool.

bookfairs.scholastic.co.uk – Run your own Scholastic Book Fair.

bookfairs.scholastic.co.uk/business_school – Find everything you need to run your own Scholastic Business School.

www.tunecore.com – Create an enterprise and sell music online.

kdp.amazon.com/self-publishing/help – Publish your very own ebook.

writers.scholastic.co.uk – Print your own book using Scholastic's We Are Writers self-publication programme.

Reports

Economics, Business and Enterprise Education: A Summary of Inspection Evidence (Ofsted, ref no. 100086, 2011).

Books

Cooperative Learning in the Classroom: Putting it into Practice by Wendy Jolliffe (Sage).

Show Me The Money: Putting the FUN into Finance! by Alvin Hall (Dorling Kindersley).

Real-Life Maths (Ages 5–7, 7–9, 9–11) by Paul Hollin (Scholastic).

Television

Young Apprentice (BBC)

Glossary

Account – an agreement between the bank and the customer for the holding of funds. An account is stored along with the person's name and unique account number.

Account number – this is a unique number that identifies the account details of the banking customer. It is a very private number that should be known only to the owner of the money in the account.

Balance – this is the total amount of money you have in your account.

Bank run (a run on the bank) – when a large number of customers withdraw their deposits from a bank or financial institution because they lose faith in it and believe it to be unstable. This can lead to a bank running out of cash and facing bankruptcy. A run on many banks at the same time results in a bank panic or financial crisis.

Capital – an accumulation of wealth.

Charity – something given to help a person or persons in need.

Coinage – the lowest denominations or parts of a denomination used within a financial zone.

Communication – the exchange of information between people, usually spoken or written.

Confidence – a belief in your ability to succeed.

Creativity – the ability to use the imagination to develop new and original ideas or things.

Credit – where a buyer can take something now and pay for it at a later, agreed time.

Currency – the form of money used within a geographic or financial exchange zone.

Currency exchange – to change one type of currency into another.

I–P

Debt – an amount (it may be financial or a service or item) that is owed to another person.

Education Business Partnerships (EBPs) – government-sponsored bodies which link the worlds of business and education to offer young people a rewarding and realistic introduction to work.

Enterprise – another term for business.

Entrepreneur – a person who has created their own business.

Ethics – a system of moral principles.

Friendly society – typically an organised association of people who regularly contribute to funds for financial benefits, health or retirement plans or life assurances.

Guilloche patterns – complex patterns that feature on many notes to prevent fraud.

Hyperinflation – where inflation grossly outweighs the capacity of the currency to keep pace with the price of goods and volume of money generated.

Individual Savings Account (ISA) – an account that is tax free to a certain limit; considered a medium-term investment account.

Inflation – a persistent and accumulative rise in general prices related to an increase in volume of money, resulting in a loss of value of the currency.

Initiative – the ability to act and make decisions without the help or advice of other people.

Interest – payment for the use of loaned money, usually calculated as a percentage of the load; the measure used to demonstrate the growth of a debt.

Investments – something that money is invested into with a view to future commodity (generally referred to as 'savings' or more creatively as a 'nest egg').

Leader – somebody who guides or directs others.

Loan – an amount of money given to somebody on the condition that it will be paid back later.

Market – a communal gathering place for buying or selling; can be a collection of stalls or shops.

Marketing – a business activity used to present a product or service in such a way as to make it desirable.

Money – a particular form of currency used for financial exchange.

National Savings and Investments (NS&I) plans – these are commonly known as investment bonds but are a series of saving options that are 100 per cent secure as they are backed by the government.

Non-governmental organisation (NGO) – generally a charity (such as Oxfam or UNICEF) working within a country to provide the type of support that a government typically would but is unable to, often due to extreme events such as civil war, drought or famine.

Poverty – a state of being poor, and in many cases of being affected by a general shortage.

Product – something made or created, generally for sale.

Repayment – paying back money that is owed to somebody.

Resilience – the ability to recover quickly from setbacks.

Risk – the statistical chance that something might go wrong or right.

Savings – a commonplace term used to describe an amount of money invested into saving, typically a bank or savings account, with the object of accruing money in a safe place.

Shop – a retail business selling a product or service.

Statement – this is where you keep track of how much money has been added and subtracted from your bank account on paper. You add what you deposit and subtract what you spend.

Sterling – the official economic name for the British currency.

Strapline – a catchy phrase that appears below a main headline.

Sweatshop – a factory where forced labour is used to create products.

Teamwork – cooperative effort by a group or team.

Trust accounts – long-term investment accounts usually involving small contributions over a long period of time (for example, £25 every month for 10 years).

Index

account 51
account numbers 51
accountants 129, 130
addition 35–6
advertising 128, 129, 130
Africa 11
allotments 81
Amazon™ 40
The Apprentice 83
art 100
auctions 132
Australia 13

balance 51, 53
bank notes 13, 14, 15, 18, 20, 27
Bank of America 51
Bank of England 6, 14, 50, 65
bank robberies 52
bank runs 52, 70–1, 73
bank statements 50, 51, 53
banking 49–53
    history 49–50
    interest 58–62
    resources 67
    savings 54–8
    sensitive issues 52
bartering 11
Becta 39
bills of exchange 59–60
book fairs 125–31

books 40
borrowing 58–62
Boxing Day Tsunami 70
breakfast events 132
British Museum 11
browsing supervisors 128, 130
budgets 22
business opportunities 107, 110
business plans 91

cafes 32, 33, 36
Cambridge Primary Review (CPR) 7
Canada 73
capital 99
carrier bags 41, 45
charitable donations 74
charity
    choosing 76–9
    definition 73
    ethics and 69–75
    fundraising 80–6
    resources 86–7
    sensitive issues 74
cheques 17
Chiddingstone Stores and Post Office 33
child sponsorship 78
Children in Need 80–1, 85
Children's Centres 79

children's savings 54–5, 56–7
China 12, 13, 27
chocolate 44
chunking skills 36
Churchill, Winston 97
Clarke MP, Charles 7
codes of conduct 75
coffee 44
coffeehouses 33
coinage 12, 13, 14, 20
    pre-decimalisation 16
commemorative coins 12–13
communication 104, 107, 109, 112
community 37, 70, 72
community charities 77–8
community projects 82–4
community values 74–5
confidence 99
creativity 95, 100, 108, 113
credit 58, 59–60
credit cards 17, 58, 59, 60
credit columns 53
currency 11–12, 13, 14
    around the world 25–9
    local currencies 27–8
currency exchange 26, 27, 29
currency world map 28
current accounts 54
customer service 128, 129, 130

Davies, Howard 91
debit cards 17
debit columns 53
debts 7, 52, 60, 63–7
    definition 64
    loans 58–62
decimalisation 16

decimals 17, 25, 35–6, 38
demand 118
Department for Children Schools and Families (DCSF) 92
Department for Education and Skills (DfES) 91
design and technology 101
Developing Enterprising Young People (Ofsted) 91
Diamond Jubilee 12
displays 128, 129, 130
drama 101

economic well-being 7
Economics, Business and Enterprise Education (Ofsted) 104, 133
economies of scale 20–1
Education Business Partnerships (EBPs) 103–5
Elizabeth II 18, 20, 28–9
English 101
enterprise
    in education 96–101
    enterprise education 91–6
    enterprise teams 124–32
    explanation 89–91
    future of 133–6
    gap between schools and enterprise 102–5
    getting started 107–14
    goes wrong 5–6
    lesson planning 114–17
    organisation 118–24
    resources 105, 136
enterprise projects 82–4
enterprising schools 94
enterprising students 94

ch–en

Index

enterprising teachers 93–4
entrepreneurship 90, 92
environment 41
ethics 70–1, 72, 73
euros 16, 25–6
events coordinators 128, 129, 130
Every Child Matters (ECM) 7
Excellence and Enjoyment 7
exchange rates 26, 29

factories 43
Fairtrade 42, 44, 45–6
farmers' markets 38
financial crises 6–7, 51, 73, 89
financial education 8–9
food miles 44
food shopping 41–2, 44–6
forgery 15, 18, 20, 21
Friendly Societies 55
fundraising 71, 80–6, 131

garment industry 43
Gates, Bill 73
geography 44, 45, 100, 123
global marketplace 41–2, 45
gold 18, 50
Gold Certificate 18
gold standard 14
greed 71
Greeks 12
A Guide to Enterprise Education (DCSF) 92
Guilloche patterns 15, 18

Hadrian, Emperor 12
haggling 37, 38
Hanging Gardens of Babylon 11

Herodotus 12
history 100
home corners 21, 31–2, 35
hyperinflation 15, 18

ICT 134, 135
illegal practice 19
Individual Savings Accounts (ISAs) 54, 55
inflation 15, 18
initiative 105
interest 58–62
    sensitive issues 60
interest rates 6, 15, 65, 66
international charities 72, 74, 77–8
International Primary Curriculum (IPC) 115–16
international schools 78
internet 135
internet banking 17, 50–1
internet safety 39–40
internet shopping 40–41
interviews 118–19, 127, 131–2
inventories 128, 130
investments 55
IT 123
It's a Wonderful Life 70

Japan 6
job descriptions 126

knowing yourself 107, 111

leadership 95, 107, 111–12
Learning to be Enterprising (Ofsted) 94–5
Little Espresso Co. 33
loans 23, 49, 58–62

definition 59
local currencies 27–8
London Olympics 12

Make Poverty History 65
Managed Learning
  Environments (MLEs) 72
managers 127–8, 129, 130
market research 118, 122
marketing 99, 107, 109–10,
  119
markets 37–9
  global marketplace 41–2
maths 17, 25, 32, 34–6, 38,
  61–2, 100, 123
McDonald's 33
menus 36–7
Merchant of Venice 65
Mesopotamia 11
metals 13, 18
MicroSociety program 103–4
mint 12
money
  around the world 25–9
  explanation 14–29
  history 11–14
  resources 29
  sensitive issues 19
moneylending 49
Morocco 14
MP3s 20–1
multiplication 36
music 134, 135

national charities 76–7
national debts 63, 65
National Savings and
  Investments (NS&I) 54
needs/wants 24, 66

negotiation 37
Nigeria 20
Nissan Motor Manufacturing
  (UK) Ltd 102–3
non-governmental
  organisations (NGOs) 73
Northern Rock 52

Ofsted 91, 94–5, 104
online banking 17, 50–1
online shopping 39–41
Operation Christmas Child 79
overdrafts 50

packaging 41, 47
Paine, Lynne Sharp 75
paper 20
paper money (see bank notes)
ParentPay® 17
Paterson, William 50
PE 101
pennies 18
percentages 59, 61, 62
Philippines 27
'pick your own' farms 38
piggy banks 54, 56
Pizza Hut 40
plastic bags 41, 45
PlayPumps 77–8
pocket money 24–5
pounds sterling 18, 20
poverty 19, 42, 43, 64, 65
Premium Bonds 54
pricing 119
product development 107,
  108–9
products 32
profits 82–3, 119–20
pyramids of Giza 11

raw materials 46
RE 100–1
receipts 32, 34–5
recessions 19
Red Nose Day 80, 85–6
repayments 59
resilience 95
responsibility 118–19
restaurants 32, 36–7
risk 95, 108, 113–14
Romania 13
Romans 12
rotas 120
rounding 36
Royal British Legion 76–7

sales 15–16
savings 54–8
    sensitive issues 56
savings accounts 54, 61–2
Scholastic Book Fairs 125–31
school councils 22, 90
school values 72–3, 75
science 100, 123
seasonal food 44
Securitas heist 52
self-publishing 134, 136
Sheba, Queen of 12
shopping
    environmental impact 41
    markets 37–9
    online shopping 39–41
    resources 47
    sensitive issues 33
    trends 41–7
    where to shop 31–7
shops 32, 33
Signposts to Safety (Becta) 39
silver 18

Smith, Adam 71
Solomon 12
St Paul's C of E Primary School
    81–4
Starbucks 33
sterling 18, 20
straplines 108, 109
sugar 44, 46
summer fairs 132
supermarkets 32, 44
sweatshops 43, 44

tallymen 60
teamwork 95, 107, 110
theft 26
Trust accounts 54, 55
tuck shops 121–4

United States 18, 25, 27–8, 51,
    56, 60, 74

value 16, 17, 37
Visual-Auditory-Kinaesthetic
    environments 95
volunteers 126–7

Wall Street 70
wars 13
watermarks 15, 28–9
whole-school approach 97–8
William III 50
work-related learning 92–3
Worldwide Christian Schools®
    78

Young Apprentice 6, 121

Zimbabwe 27